GW00391531

Viking

Book 1 of the '*Viking Ventures*' series

by Ole Åsli and Tony Bakkejord

www.vikingauthors.com

Cover design by Maria Gamst

www.gamstdesign.no

Copyright © 2020 by Envig AS

ISBN: 978-82-93794-98-1 (e-book)

ISBN: 978-82-93794-96-7 (paperback)

ISBN: 978-82-93794-93-6 (hardcover)

NORÐREYJAR

SANDAY

SUÐREYJAR

PICCLAND

NORTHUMBRIA

WUCESTRE

IRELAND

KELLS

LINN DUACHAILL

DYFLIN

MERCIA

WESSEX

Chapter 1: Marcus

Northumbria, September 841

'Raid or trade?'

Standing on the pier, Marcus watched the two ships, which had appeared at dawn, heading towards the village of Wucestre at the mouth of the River Wansbeck. Fast, elegant ships, powered by both sail and oars.

The merchant's son knew them well.

His father, Gaius, was born the day Vikings raided the wealthy monastery of Lindisfarne, half a century earlier. Almost every summer since, Northmen from Horthaland had visited the towns along the coast of Northumbria. Usually, they came with trade goods and silver – sometimes, they came with swords and fire.

'What more do we have to offer?' his father asked quietly.

Wucestre had been a thriving trading town, until a rainy morning three winters past, when heathens found plundering preferable to trading. Everyone lost loved ones that day as they were either slaughtered or captured as slaves.

Now, most buildings lay abandoned as many of those who had survived took their meagre belongings and found work in the coal mines to the north. Trade had since subsided, and Wucestre was now but a poor village.

Marcus looked around, taking stock of his surroundings. He opened his mouth, about to respond 'Nothing' but stopped short when he realised he was wrong. He exhaled slowly. The obvious answer escaped in a low voice:

'Slaves.'

His father had already turned to go and barked a brief command over his shoulder.

'Bring Julia to safety!'

Julia was Marcus's sister, younger by two winters. The once cheerful girl had turned quiet and withdrawn in recent years. Since the loss of their mother, she rarely expressed any joy or passion. Tall and slender, she would soon be a grown woman. Many found her attractive, but her stern countenance made even grown men shy away.

The Vikings would not be shy.

Marcus opened the door the same moment the church bell started chiming. He found Julia at work, as usual.

'Vikings!' he said as soon as he entered. 'We must leave. Now!'

Julia stiffened and drew a breath. Looking up at Marcus, she nodded silently. The girl picked up a knife and a waterskin and draped a blanket over her shoulders. Without a backward glance, she marched out the door and sped up the road alongside the river.

Marcus watched Julia's diminishing silhouette as she disappeared, admiring her determination. Snapping back to reality, he found the small hand axe he used for cleaving kindling – Julia might need it. Keeping the heavy woodman's axe for himself, he gathered what little food he could find and packed it into his thick winter cloak. Nothing short of divine intervention would allow him to eat again – this day or any other day. He broke into a run to catch up with his sister.

He passed dozens of villagers on the road, most of whom were women and children. Some not much younger than he was. The women threw nervous gazes in the direction of the ships heading towards the beach. Despite their mother's efforts to remain calm, most of the children were crying, their eyes large with fear.

Marcus found Julia at the head of the pack. She walked fast, without looking back or talking to anyone. They strode side by side for a while, the silence between them growing louder. What advice could he offer? How far could the women flee? Would the heathens seek them out further inland to take more slaves? Would they return whence they came after laying waste to the village or remain indefinitely to plunder the surrounding areas?

He placed a hand on her forearm.

'I have to go back.'

Julia continued walking but turned her gaze towards him.

'Do you?' Her voice reminded Marcus of how young she was.

'The men are gathering to launch a counter-attack or at least stave them off long enough for you to get away,' he replied. 'This time, I have to be a part of it.'

'How much time can you buy me with your life, brother?'

Marcus was strong and agile, as most males in his family had been. Nevertheless, he had yet to reach manhood and never had any combat training. Still, he knew how to swing an axe, and often imagined himself in the heat of battle when he felled a tree. On the other hand, he never used the axe for anything but trees. And trees never fought back.

How long could he survive an encounter with a seasoned warrior? A warrior whose training began from the very day he learned how to walk? And with a bloodied history of having slain many men? What if two or more cornered him? He might be able to parry the first blow or at best two, but it would be over before it really began.

He had no answer. Instead, Marcus grabbed his sister's hand and pulled her to his side.

'You do understand, don't you?' he whispered as he hugged her. There was no sound, just tears – the first he had seen since that awful morning three winters ago.

Marcus hung the hand axe from the rope tied around her waist and gave her the cloak and the food. She accepted it without taking her eyes off him.

'Come and find me, brother,' she said. 'Promise me!'

'Of course,' Marcus replied, 'I'll find you when they are gone.'

He laid his hands on her shoulders and met her gaze before giving her a peck on her forehead. Without another word, he released her and set off in the opposite direction of the crowd who were hurrying to escape. Through the tears, he recognised his friends, their siblings, and mothers. A gut-wrenching feeling told him he would never see them again.

As Marcus returned to his home, war cries from the assaulting heathens blended with the screams of the terrified townspeople. His father had already donned several layers of his thickest clothing and tightened the belt with his gladius. He had always been proud of his Roman lineage, even though the Roman governors and their legions left the province of Britannia hundreds of years ago. For centuries, it had been a family tradition to give their children Roman names. Gaius had spent many nights telling stories and teaching his children Latin, as his father had taught him and his forefathers before him.

Marcus could understand Latin prayers, but he had yet to carry a conversation in Latin with anyone outside the family. He also doubted that the short, double-edged sword his father had polished, sharpened and practised with when he thought no one was watching, indeed was a gladius as used by the legionaries. It was certainly not six hundred years old. More likely, it was an exotic short sword one of his not-too-distant ancestors had acquired in a trade deal with some Saracen merchants.

Marcus checked the knife hanging from his belt and picked up the woodman's axe. He felt something was lacking, as if getting dressed and equipped for battle should take more time. However, he did not have any armour, helmet or shield. There was nothing more to do.

Marcus heard the screams of men as axes or spears struck them. The same sounds he had heard three years ago. It dawned on him that what remained of his life was to run past the six houses separating them and the pier swarming with invaders only to be struck down in a matter of moments.

He tried to walk to the door, but his body would not obey.

His father's face was calm and gentle when he laid his hands on Marcus's shoulders.

'Do what you have to do, my boy,' he said softly, hugging Marcus against his chest. Then he turned and went out the door.

Marcus glanced out the door and saw his father draw the sword and start running towards the pier, where death awaited him.

Marcus turned away. Just as he had done three years earlier, he looked towards the trapdoor. Underneath was a small cellar his father had dug six or seven winters ago after marauding Vikings had wiped out several villages along the coast. Gaius initially intended to dig an escape tunnel, but the loose earth had forced him to stop digging before it collapsed and brought the house down with it.

Marcus and Julia had hidden in the cellar the day the Northmen attacked. There was room for their mother too, but she decided to stay behind to cover the hatch, so invaders would not find the children. She held one finger to her mouth, urging them to keep quiet as she shut the trapdoor.

Moments later, the heathens found her.

Marcus had sat in the dark holding Julia throughout the day and night that followed. They smelled smoke and burning wood and heard the sounds of trampling feet, swords against swords and axes against shields. Desperate wails and laments mixed with the roaring cheers of the victors, as their neighbours were slaughtered or enslaved.

Now, it was happening again. Marcus grabbed a blanket and a waterskin before lifting the trapdoor. The familiar scent of moist soil filled his nostrils. The feelings of distress and memories from three years before came flooding back, overwhelming him. Loaded with fear and shame, he climbed down into the dark cellar.

Chapter 2: Ulv

'I'm dead.'

The young Northman, Ulv, shook his head and wondered how his plan had gone so wrong. Standing by the mast on one of the two ships gliding swiftly over the water, he watched the town they were about to pillage. A river divided the village into two parts. The south bank nestled a mill and a dozen other buildings, including a large stone house with a bell tower that loomed a few man-lengths over the rooftops.

Most of the buildings stood on the north bank, several already missing their ceilings or parts of the walls. Along the river, twenty larger stone houses with peat-covered roofs huddled. Ulv noticed two figures standing on the stone pier that extended into the ocean. Between the buildings and the ships was a sandy beach, a belt of head-sized rocks tracing above the watermark. The band of dark sand coloured the shoreline, half the distance between the rocks and the water, a telltale sign the tide had fallen.

A third ship had laid a different course and disembarked on the southernmost side of the river during the night, allowing the crew with the dogs to venture inland to cut off and capture anyone who tried to escape. Sigurd Jarl and Magnus Trygg's ships were to attack between ótta and daybreak, surprising the sleeping townspeople. They arrived later than intended, as the buildings bathed in the soft light of the morning sun. Behind wooden crates and under the coarse cloth coverings, the warriors kept out of sight.

Sigurd Jarl anticipated that their soon-to-be victims would remain hopeful the Northmen came with silver. Soon, his men would throw themselves over the oars and row full speed towards the beach. By then, it would be too late for the unsuspecting peasants and fishermen to organise any semblance of defence, let alone any attempts to flee.

Ulv glanced at the warriors who were making their final preparations for battle. Those not manning the oars were making their final preparations for battle, slapping their faces or muttering prayers to the gods. The Jarl sat grooming his hair and beard with a bone comb. Black hair frosted with grey stripes and a full beard kept short to frame the pig-like face that mounted a pair of close-set eyes and a small mouth with crooked teeth. A scruffy one-eyed tomcat with a stump of a tail lay curled in his lap.

Ulv was too concerned about his immediate future to focus on the others. He was not a warrior. Even if he was to die in battle, he doubted the gods would give him a seat in Valhall, and neither would they need him in Ragnarok. The plan had been to prove that Ulv's non-warlike skills could be an asset to the Jarl. It had not worked – not at all.

Many of the Jarl's men deemed Ulv lucky to be granted the chance to redeem himself. In reality, however, this was no chance at all. How could he prove his worth as a warrior? How would he survive? For a brief moment, he wished he were among the Northumbrians running for the dubious safety of the woods.

War cries were ringing in Ulv's ears as he jumped ashore and ran towards the buildings of the village. The Jarl led the charge, but the massive chieftain could not keep up the pace and was soon overtaken by the berserks and warriors in the prime of their youth.

A few dozen townsmen had rallied to form a desperate wall of defence between the stone buildings. The Northmen assumed their battle formation, favouring to fight in small groups of two to three warriors. A warrior with a long spear provided the lead support for two other melee fighters wielding shields and axes or swords.

A few steps ahead, a scowling Kjetil Korte turned back to face him. 'Come on, whelp, make yourself useful for once!'

He shouted for everyone to hear – for the Jarl to hear. He was not wearing his helmet, and his long golden hair beat like delicate wings with every massive step. Kjetil was among those who decidedly meant that Ulv should have been punished in an entirely different way, rather than be given the opportunity to win honour and wealth on a campaign. Ulv clenched his teeth and followed Kjetil's broad, imposing figure towards the village's buildings.

Ulv waited for the right moment. He could not charge into the villagers like the others. His compatriots were all ahead of him. Their attention fixed on their unfortunate victims. Ulv looked around before he disappeared around a corner and slipped further away from the battle.

Taking a look over his shoulder, he witnessed Magnus Trygg thrusting the edge of his shield into the head of his adversary before lashing the sword into the victim's knee. It looked simple, almost half-hearted. A routine executed hundreds of times before.

Ulv shifted his focus back to himself. He did not believe anyone had seen him, as they appeared wholly devoted to stamping out the little resistance the villagers posed. He paused against the wall of a low stone building, trying to think. The words of Kjetil Korte still rang in his head: 'Make yourself useful …' Ulv considered returning to the fray. He could probably avoid being killed by the villagers, amidst the violent and dominant warriors from the north. Nevertheless, his participation would count for as little as nothing, and he would still be rendered useless in the eyes of his kinsmen.

He regretted having left his bow on the ship. With it, he could join in the battle from a distance. Even shooting at men entangled in close combat, he should be able to hit his marks. However, one unexpected move could make him miss his shot and injure one of his own. Besides, it would not be deemed manly to use the bow after the melee had begun. Useful, maybe. Honourable? Hardly.

Perhaps he could escape by fleeing into the forest as the villagers had done. Flee, with those who were incapable or did not possess the courage to fight, such as the women and the children. And then what? He might not feel at home or accepted among the Vikings, but Northumbrians would consider him an outright enemy.

'Stop and fight, you cowardly rat!'

The roar pulled Ulv out his reverie. Someone came running. He took a step forward and glanced around the corner. There was nobody there – he turned.

The next moment, a man sagged to the ground, and Ulv felt warm blood spreading over his hand.

The world stood still. Ulv watched his hand holding on to the bloody knife that slowly slipped out of the elderly man's stomach as he slumped quietly to the ground. Ulv could not remember carrying the sax, the long knife, in his hand. The man's short, double-edged sword clattered as it fell to the ground. The lifeless hand bore an old signet ring. Dark eyes stared blankly at him. Ulv looked down at the man – staring for a thousand heartbeats, or was it ten?

Maybe not even that.

Kjetil Korte towered over him. The giant glowered at Ulv, his teeth clenched, his polished sword levelled with his shoulders. Through his shock, Ulv barely perceived Kjetil saying something incomprehensible about stealing from him. He had not stolen anything but discerned he was not being accused of taking any of the man's possessions. The moment he realised the weight of the situation, it was almost too late. Kjetil Korte held his body perfectly balanced, the left foot a little in front of the other. His sword arm raised high and a resolute look in his eyes.

The sword swung down diagonally against Ulv's unprotected head with a stroke that would have split his skull in two. Narrowly ducking under the blow, Ulv rolled backwards and bolted in the opposite direction as soon as his feet hit the ground.

Darting between dying villagers, bloodstained Northmen and small houses, he jumped a fence and slipped under an old cart that was missing a wheel. The sounds of the pursuit had faded. Looking back, he saw no signs of them.

What now? The villagers were overwhelmed, the fighting would soon be over, and Ulv's chances of leaving this place with the slightest trace of honour were fast disappearing. Sporadic cries from villagers mixed with triumphant cheers from the Vikings as the would-be slaves were roughly gathered and bound.

Shouts from a particular pack of warriors rose above everyone else's. They were the Jarl's berserks. A young Northman, wielding a sword and an axe, led the attack upon the remaining pocket of resistance. He moved gracefully, like a seasoned performer of a deadly dance. His otherwise bared upper body was draped in a wolf's pelt.

It was said that the berserks mastered rune magic, but Ulv had not witnessed any magic. Not since his father revealed his tricks were just that, mere tricks. The berserks were skilled warriors, mad as dogs and strong as bears, with ruthless aggression and no fear. So very different from him.

Blocking the berserks from his mind, he moved further away from the battle. Soon, he noticed a small house with the door left ajar. He stalked past a barrel filled with rainwater and slid through the opening. Someone shouted as he closed the door behind him. Fearing he had been spotted, he leaned his back against the door, his failing courage limiting his actions to wishing and hoping.

Several shouts nearby made him hold his breath, listening. Then, he heard a scratching sound just outside the door. A sound similar to when his father pulled logs to the hewing stump. Still leaning against the door, he briefly examined the room. It was apparent that a family had lived there. There was a small table with four chairs, a bench and some simple cooking appliances. In the corner, partially concealed by the table, he spotted a trapdoor.

He looked for a place to hide when he heard a familiar voice, just outside the door. Kjetil Korte yelled.

'Nothing there. Burn it down!'

Fear clutched Ulv's chest like a clawed hand of a draugr. They are burning the houses!

Soon after, Sigurd Jarl answered:

'You heard him, torch it.'

Ulv tentatively pushed against the door. It was stuck. He shoved harder but to no avail. When he heard the crackling of the flames consuming the peat on the roof, he retreated three steps before slamming his shoulder against the door. He might as well try to unbalance a jotne.

His back against the door, he slumped to the floor. The flames broke through the meshwork of branches in the roof. The first waves of heat pricked his skin, and the smoke singed in his chest as he inhaled.

He should have taken his chances in battle, but the choice was no longer his to make. Cold despair struck his stomach like a hammer as he realised that his final moments had come. The thought of the afterlife provided no comfort. Burning to death, in a remote and unfamiliar house, was not an honourable death.

The gods would not be pleased.

Chapter 3: Cellar

Marcus crouched in the dark. He no longer reacted to the sounds of fighting and killing outside, but he knew all too well what was going on. The Vikings had slaughtered the village men who had sacrificed their lives to give their women and children a chance. Now, the heathen ran with bloody axes and swords from building to building, in search of prey.

Several of the rich monasteries in the region had been looted in the last fifty years. There, the heathen could fill the ships with relics of gold, jewelled books and chests. In a village like Wucestre, few assets would be of interest. But the Vikings could make a nice profit at the slave markets in Hedeby or Seville if they captured a young woman or a strong man.

Marcus froze when he heard footsteps on the wooden planks that covered the dirt floor overhead. He had no hope that the hostile pagans would see any value in young men hiding in basements. Resisting the urge to pull the blanket over him like a frightened child, he pulled the knife as quietly as he could.

It was quiet for a short while. Then followed several dull thuds from the room above, and creaking as someone moved around on the planks. Quiet again. Suddenly, the trapdoor was lifted, and through the opening, Marcus saw the silhouette of a man against the flames. The wood crackled and burned, and it smelled of sour smoke. Before he could figure out how to deal with the house burning, a more imminent threat emerged: the figure crawled down into the cellar and closed the hatch above him.

Marcus had cowered in the cellar for long enough for his eyes to adjust to the darkness. Before the guest appeared, he had been able to see the earth walls and support beams. He considered stabbing with his knife before the other was alerted to his presence. Whoever landed the first blow would have a vital advantage, no matter where it hit.

Uncertainty over the intruder's identity made him hesitate. Ravaging heathens were unlikely to hide in cellars. It was far more plausible that one of his neighbours was seeking sanctuary. Perhaps even his father? No, Gaius had been so proud when he equipped his sword, accepting his fate.

In the glow of the flames, where light and shadow danced around each other, Marcus could see that this was no villager. A fair-haired man, with narrow eyes that strained to see in the dark. He had no helmet but wore a thick coat of arms on his upper body. In his hand, he held a bloody knife, pointing at Marcus.

Marcus could not read the facial expression in the dancing shadows. The man did not behave like someone who wanted to kill everything he saw, but his watchful eyes, tense body and bloody knife testified that he could very well kill. One who would do whatever necessary to survive. He did not understand why the young man was sitting here, but there were more important things to think about: the house above was on fire.

'Help us …?' Marcus asked in as gentle a voice as he could, in what he hoped was the language of the Northmen.

Marcus had a strong suspicion that his choice of words was not the best, but hoped the Viking would appreciate his intentions. Slowly, he lowered his knife. The fair-haired intruder examined him in silence for a short while, then nodded. Marcus tentatively placed two fingers on the hand holding the long knife, feeling the sticky blood on his fingertips. Warily, the Viking also lowered his blade to the ground.

Marcus leaned forward and opened the trapdoor. A wave of heat from the burning roof and walls washed against his face. The house was full of smoke, but along the floor he could see the lower part of the door. He retreated to the cellar, grabbed the water skin, and handed the blanket to the fair-haired young man. The Viking accepted it with a curious expression on his face. Marcus opened the waterskin and poured its contents on the wool cloth.

The Northman pointed to his chest and said: 'Ulv.'

Marcus emptied the water skin before returning the gesture. 'Marcus.'

He picked up his axe and climbed up. The room was full of flakes of burning peat and wood. Along the walls, the flames had spread to the floorboards. With his head low, he crawled to the door on his knees and elbows. Marcus inhaled, got up on one knee and struck a few blows with the axe against the door. The heat and smoke forced him back down. Lying with his face against the floorboards, he dropped the axe and coughed to clear his lungs of the acrid smoke. There was a cool reprieve as the wet blanket enveloped his back, and soon he heard the sounds of splintering wood as the Northman hacked at the door with the axe.

Chapter 4: Julia

Julia slowed down. Terrified mothers and children passed her as she tried to regain control of her breathing and her thoughts. They trotted up the road along the north side of the river and looked back over their shoulders. Julia stopped, turned around and saw men with axes and swords running between the buildings.

She had done this so many times before. Every night, ever since the day the Vikings took mother, she had pondered what she should have done instead of hiding in the cellar. What would she do if the Vikings returned?

Now they were here again, and she tried to recall the plans she had made when she lay safely in bed.

She was not tempted to hide in the cellar again. Her memories from three years earlier were too painful. Furthermore, the trapdoor was not hard to find, and Vikings were in the habit of setting houses on fire. The thought of sitting under the floor while the house above was on fire, did not appeal to her.

Julia had fantasised about finding a weapon and resisting, avenging the abduction of her mother. Now, she realised it would never be possible. They were too many, and too powerful. And she was too afraid to face them.

The only escape was into the forest, away from the sea and the ships. Even that could go wrong. The last time the Vikings attacked, some warriors with dogs had disembarked on the south bank of the river during the night, and crossed it further upstream. There, they waited. The villagers had fled straight into their trap. The foremost had run up the road, and everyone else had followed, like sheep. Everyone ran. Nobody stopped to think.

Many who tried to hide in the forest had been found by the Vikings' huge, grey dogs. A woman and a young boy had escaped by throwing themselves into the river and swimming underwater with the current until they could land on the south bank. The woman had died in childbirth last winter. The boy was now among the men who were preparing to be slaughtered.

Julia considered swimming across to the south bank of the great river but gave up the idea. The Vikings could be waiting on the other side, or she might be pulled with the current down towards the village. Even if she succeeded in crossing the river unseen, her clothes would be wet, making it even harder to get through the night without fire or shelter.

She decided that her best chance was to leave the road before the ford and escape into the forest. If she crossed the shallow tributaries a few times, it would be difficult for the dogs to follow her. Marcus had told of an abandoned hut she could reach before evening if she headed for the marshes to the north-west. There, she could seek shelter for the night.

She unfolded the cloak and wrapped the blanket and the food in it. Then, she tied the corners together making it easier to carry. The hunting knife hung by her right hip, the small axe by her left. She attached the small dagger to her left forearm, inside her sleeve, and threw the bundle over her shoulder. Her preparations done, she followed a woman with three children for a while. As they passed a part of the forest where the vegetation was dense, she left the road and pushed through the bushes. There she waited a bit, to make sure no one was following her. It pained her to leave her neighbours to their own fates, but she stood a better chance of not being found if she was alone. From a distance, the clangs of metal against metal reached her.

Julia turned away for the last time and walked into the woods.

She had been there many times, but had never thought about how much noise she made. Branches snapped, her breath sounded like a gale, and her heart pounded like the hooves of a galloping horse. She could not decide whether to run to get as far away as she could, or tread carefully to make as little noise as possible. She landed on a compromise. Walking fast, while trying to bend away bushes and branches without breaking them. She found a rhythm she could keep without getting too tired, and soon she heard no other sounds than the soft rush of a river further ahead. No sounds, in a forest full of animals and birds? She stopped and turned in the direction she was coming from. There was a faint waft of smoke, but no sounds. No, there was something. A shout? A male voice? It came from the forest, not down from the river.

They were after her!

Julia set off without concern for tracks or noises. The voice boomed again, and a dog barked. If she crossed the river, the animal would lose her scent. Wet clothes were the least of her worries.

The river was about five man-lengths wide. She did not know how deep it was, but there was no time to look for another place to cross. Lifting the bundle over her head, she waded into the river. The cold water reached her hips before she had taken three steps. Halfway across, the water reached her chest, and the current pulled at her with invisible tendrils.

To her relief, the current decreased as she approached the riverbank. Julia grabbed a branch and pulled herself out of the water. Soaked, she climbed ashore. Luckily, the bundle with the food was still dry. She took a few deep breaths and ran on. Shrubs scratched her legs, and branches whipped her face. The wet tunic wrapped around her legs and made her stumble several times.

Had the dogs lost her scent? A little further, and she would have shaken them off. She slowed down and searched for a place to hide. The breath tore in her chest, and her skin was cold. Could she stop and wrap the blanket around herself to get warm again? No, she had to get further away.

Julia was about to set the pace again when she heard a rustle behind her. As she turned, she looked straight into a row of stained teeth. A large, grey dog came rushing towards her.

She managed to pull the hunting knife and get her arms up before the dog slammed into her. The canine's speed and weight knocked her backwards, and she landed on her back on the ground. Then followed a crack and a sharp whimper, and a flood of pain from her left arm.

The dog lay on the ground behind her, its jaws still clutching her arm. Blood pumped from the gash in the dog's throat. The beast drew a few shuddering breaths, then expired next to the bloody knife.

Carefully, Julia extricated her arm from between the hound's teeth. The pain pounded with every heartbeat and intensified with every movement. One or both bones in her left underarm was broken, and blood seeped from many wounds. The bundle and the dagger she had tied to her forearm, had limited the extent of the injuries. Nevertheless, she knew all too well that many had died in pain and fever after being bitten by animals. The bleeding had to be stopped, and the fracture splinted. Julia searched the ground for something she could use. Her gaze stopped at a pair of shoes. Wet leather shoes. She looked up at a large man with a yellow beard.

Something slammed into her head, and the man disappeared.

Chapter 5: Envig

Ulv and Marcus broke through the wreckage of the door. Exhausted, singed and gasping for air, they managed a few unsteady steps before collapsing in front of the burning house. Ulv did not notice the men before he and Marcus were lifted up and dragged away by four of the Jarl's berserks. No match for their strength, Ulv focused instead on catching his breath. Eventually, the smell of salt sea overcame the scent of burnt wood, and below him trampled soil gradually gave way to wet sand.

'Look what came crawling out of a hole!' one of the berserks said as they dumped Ulv and Marcus in front of the Jarl's feet. The chieftain was examining the loot they had gathered, accompanied by the thrall who Ulv knew as Emil.

Kjetil Korte closed the distance between himself and Ulv with long steps, drawing his massive sword as he advanced.

'The bastard stole my kill from right in front of me. I'll destroy him!'

If nothing else, Kjetil was predictable. Ulv got up on his knees and spat.

'I have not taken anything that is yours! I killed an enemy who came running against me!' Ulv lowered his voice. 'At least I did not try to kill one of my own. At least I did not try to kill my brother!'

'You're not my brother!' Kjetil said, but the expression on his face was more hesitant this time. Ulv saw an opening.

'Not by blood, no. But before we sailed, the Jarl proclaimed that all who sailed together were brothers. There should be no quarrels between us, no fighting, no blood. We should act as one from when we set out until we returned. I was there, too. If you kill me, you shall bring shame and dishonour to us all.'

Kjetil faltered for an instant, casting a stunned glance first at the Jarl, then back to Ulv. His rage bubbled up again, and he raised his sword.

'Stop,' Sigurd Jarl said. 'Enough!' The second order louder and more commanding. 'The boy has a point, even though he is indeed pushing his luck.'

'Envig?' Magnus Trygg suggested settling the conflict by one-on-one combat, a duel.

'It is much more than the gnome deserves,' Kjetil asserted.

The Jarl turned towards Ulv, who was standing up again.

So be it, a fight I cannot possibly win is the best I can get out of this situation, thought Ulv. He said: 'But if I win, I am a free man.'

The Jarl nodded. Ulv tilted his head sideways at Marcus.

'And he is mine.' He looked at the Jarl, who hesitated long enough for Ulv to add, 'And we shall be safe from my brothers until we are home!'

Slowly, Sigurd Jarl raised his hand. 'So be it. Envig! To first blood. And the conditions are as stated.'

'When I win, the thrall will be mine,' Kjetil concluded with satisfaction.

*

Looking down upon his trembling hands, Ulv had yet to regain his composure after barely escaping from that blazing house. He felt feverish. The scent of residual smoke still clung to him, his skin hot and his eyes stung. He was ashamed of his fear. Everything was spiralling out of control, even more so since the meeting with the Jarl and Kjetil Korte. Still, he was glad he was not cleaved in two on the spot. Another predicament had presented itself, and he was now destined to face the raid's most experienced warrior head-to-head. All he did was postpone the inevitable. Only now, alone with his thoughts, did he have the time to take it all in. His heart thumped, and his breathing was laboured as though the fight had already begun. His feet were cold and his mouth dry. He was certainly not in control, not one bit. Ulv looked around, and had an urge to run. Could he escape?

The men around him bustled as they occupied themselves with the preparations for the coming fight. In a suitable area on the beach, between the water and the stones where the ground was level, they formed a makeshift arena by laying their cloaks on the sand. Others stood talking and laughing in small groups. Nobody seemed to care about him nor his fate.

Ulv gazed at the villager called Marcus. His face was white and speckled with black spots of soot. His wide eyes met Ulv's. For reasons unknown, the sight of this stranger somewhat calmed Ulv. Not entirely, but enough to allow him to think. He forced himself to take deep, calming breaths. The fog in his head gradually cleared, and he figured he needed to occupy himself. How had he prepared before, practising with his father?

Checking his equipment, he took off his cloak, folded it and laid it upon a stone. He examined the seax hanging from his belt. The weight of the long knife felt reassuring in his hands, and he tested the edge of the blade against his forefingers. Not that he could do anything about it if he found it to be blunt. Nevertheless, it felt good to busy himself with something other than his gloomy thoughts. Once again, Ulv took a deep breath. Father had said that it was good to be afraid before a fight, it meant that the body was poised and ready. He was still ridden by fear, but at least panic no longer controlled him.

Ulv wiped the blood from the seax with a rag and glanced at Kjetil Korte. The signet ring that the old man wore was now wrapped around Kjetil's little finger as if to emphasise his formidable girth and height. His hair was slicked back and his face, clean-shaven. A thin scar ran along the right side of his cheek. Kjetil fingered a piece of jewellery he wore under his armour. It was shaped like Thor's hammer and cut from bone. He placed it to his lips, murmured a few words and put it back. Then he put on his helmet.

Ulv had barely witnessed Kjetil in battle, but the fact that he used a sword distinguished him from most other warriors. Few could afford a sword, or were so lucky as to be rewarded one. A warrior who owned a sword would likely know well how to wield it.

This mountain of a man was unmistakably strong, and his range of attack would be vast. He carried a shield that could be used as a weapon as well as for defence. A skilled Northman could easily destroy you with his shield while you focused on his sword. A long padded coat protected the vital parts of the body. The helmet protected his skull and the ridge of his nose but did not limit his vision. The pants were thinner than the coat and would not prevent Kjetil from moving freely.

Ulv visualised the fight, creating a scene with all the details his imagination could muster. He envisaged the cloaks on the ground that marked the arena and the men gathered around. He visualised an opening in the giant's defence, and sensation as the seax tore into the warrior's flesh. Suddenly, he saw an image of himself knocked to the ground, bleeding, with Kjetil's frame towering over him. He shook his head, freeing himself from those thoughts and refocused on recalling the previous sensation he had, the feeling of victory.

He held on to this image as he walked the few steps over to the temporary arena. Kjetil was already waiting for him, shield and sword at the ready and a cold smile playing on his lips.

Ulv regarded the men encircling them. They howled and laughed, seemingly appreciating the spectacle before them. They hurled insults, some at each other, but most were directed at him. Above the commotion, Ulv picked out words of encouragement for Kjetil, but none for him. He glanced at Marcus, who crouched on his knees in front of Magnus Trygg. The veteran had placed a firm hand on the young man's neck. Ulv knew the responsibility that lay on his shoulders, that he fought for the fate of this dark-haired youngster too.

Ulv expected Kjetil to charge, wild and uncontrolled, to finish the fight as quickly as possible. However, Kjetil approach was controlled. He slashed his sword in precise arcs from side to side. Although these blows were predictable, Ulv quickly came under pressure. The arena was no more than fifteen steps from end to end, and Kjetil had an unsurpassable reach. With a sudden shift in speed, he broke his pattern. He came in high with the shield before he swung his sword low towards Ulv's legs. Ulv moved sideways at the edges of the arena. Each time Kjetil made a slash with the sword, Ulv ducked, jumped or rolled to evade. Several times, he came close to stepping out of the ring, but the spectators quickly drove him back with a kick or shove in the back. Some made clucking sounds – the insinuation was obvious.

Kjetil advanced on Ulv, alternating his attacks with different combinations. A sweeping slash high and across from the right down to the left, followed by a backhanded arc from left to right. The next attack, a quick thrust, threw Ulv off balance with nowhere to dodge. The giant was on his toes, his sword pointing skywards before the finale. The spectators shouted in excitement when the sword descended with exceptional power as to cleave Ulv down to his shoulders.

Sighs of disappointment ran through the crowd as Ulv, at the very last moment, launched himself to the side and managed to get away. Ulv was out of breath and disoriented, having exerted his energy from evading the giant's relentless attacks. To his annoyance, he never got close enough to his opponent to use his long knife.

Kjetil continued pressing the attack with vicious combinations of swift and deadly blows and thrusts, and Ulv barely hung on to his skin by jumping, dodging and moving. Each swing brought the blade closer to its target. The seasoned warrior grew more and more aggravated for every strike that did not connect with Ulv's skull. The onlookers shouted out, they too frustrated and disdained at Ulv's cowardice. Once again, Kjetil swung across from right to left. Ulv danced three steps backwards, the sword passing merely a hands-breadth from his face as it whistled through the air. He twisted away from the backhand that he anticipated would follow.

It didn't.

Instead, Kjetil smashed the boss of his shield squarely into Ulv's chest. He landed on his back among the spectators and immediately recognised the danger. Kjetil roared in triumph and chopped down at his opponent sprawling helplessly on the ground. Ulv saw his doom. There was no room to roll away from the oncoming blow. All he could do was close his eyes.

A loud metallic clang resounded, reverberating across the beach. Ulv startled. His first thought was that something shattered close to his ears. Between his ears? When he opened his eyes, he was staring straight into the inside of a shield. It was Magnus Trygg who intervened. Kjetil breathed heavily, eyes burning into Trygg.

'He's outside the arena, the victory is yours,' the seasoned warrior said calmly.

'No!' Kjetil answered. 'We fight until one of us draws blood. Does he bleed?'

'No,' came the answer from the men encircling Ulv.

Two men took hold of his arms and pulled him back into the ring. Someone threw his knife on the ground beside him. Ulv got to his feet and picked it up.

'No!' repeated Ulv, jaw clenched. He looked up at Kjetil through narrow eyes. 'To first blood.'

Magnus Trygg looked at the Jarl, who gave a short nod.

'Continue,' the Jarl said, 'but keep him in the ring.'

The warriors shouted and cheered in anticipation of a bloody conclusion. They banded closer together and held shields in front of them, forming a wooden wall around the makeshift arena.

The fight resumed. Kjetil's breathing sounded laboured. His sword hung lower, and his attacks were ever more uncontrolled. Ulv gripped the long knife until his knuckles turned white.

The large warrior took a long step forward. His shield was lowered to the side, leaving his flank unguarded. The sword sliced through the air in a horizontal arc from Ulv's left. Ulv evaded by ducking to one knee as the sword passed just over his hair. He thrust his knife, attempting to drive it deep into Kjetil's left leg. The blade hit something hard. And got stuck. Not in muscles or bone, but in Kjetil's heavy wooden shield. In a smooth motion, Kjetil jerked and twisted the shield back, along with Ulv's weapon as he lost his grip on the knife. Kjetil grinned, loosened the blade from the wood and stuck it in his belt.

There was no time to despair. Kjetil pushed forward again, and Ulv retreated with each blow. He would soon run out of space. He took a last long step backwards. The warriors behind him shouted and shoved him with their shields. Ulv leaned against one of the shields and resisted when he felt the metal boss pressing harder into his back. Kjetil was five short steps away. He held his shield out to prevent Ulv from getting away on his left side. The sword held out wide on his right and poised to swing.

Ulv felt the shield at his back give away before it was driven hard into his back again. Taking advantage of the shield's forceful momentum, he plunged forward, quickly swerving under the Kjetil's shield arm. He seized the knife hooked under the giant's belt with his left hand, rolling just before he hit the ground. As he passed under Kjetil, he swung the seax backwards and into the giant's leg.

Kjetil turned and slashed with his sword, but missed by a man's length. Ulv stared at his colossal opponent's leg. The small lapse in concentration could have been fatal. Kjetil slashed again. Ulv sprang aside and barely got away. A new wild swing from Kjetil. His face was a grimace, eyes wide, clenched teeth bared. Ulv backed away.

The blood trickling down Kjetil's leg was visible to all.

The Jarl raised his hand to halt the fight.

Ulv found himself alone while each of the men came and left after picking up their cloaks from the sand. Nobody congratulated him. Nobody spoke to him or spared a glance at him. He had just overcome their strongest warrior in a duel, but the reception he received was icy – no praise or recognition, only silence and isolation. Disappointment mingled with relief. He was happy, yet afraid, and most of all, he felt drained and exhausted. He overheard murmurs around him, most of them incomprehensible, but there were snatches of how their raid on a puny village had displeased Odin. Others muttered Loke's name under their breaths.

Ulv sat down, withdrew into his thoughts, and closed the mad world out.

Chapter 6: Trygg

Ulv observed Marcus, who was sitting with his back to the mast. The boy was soaked after a day out in the rain and wind. When the downpour came the day before, the crew had stretched a rough-spun cloth over the stern. Ulv had tried to bring his thrall under the makeshift roof, but the sharp tip of a sword against his back had told the slave that he was not welcome.

Someone threw a piece of dried meat in front of Marcus, who looked up at it. It seemed he was considering whether it was worth the effort to attempt to chew the tough meat. Finally, he reached for it, but stopped when one of the warriors picked it up in front of him. The crew chuckled. It had happened before. The thrall crouched again, with his arms around his knees.

Ulv witnessed the exchange uneasily. He felt an urge to intervene but did not know how. He barely survived the encounter with Kjetil Korte on the beach. Drawing the attention or anger of yet another one of his warmongering brethren looking for a fight would surely lower his chances of returning home alive.

'Leave it,' Magnus Trygg said, without looking up or raising his voice.

The veteran resumed his conversation with the young berserk called Vass. Ulv, eavesdropping, had been captivated by the seasoned Viking's tales of the East, the Serkland raids.

The man who had picked up the tiny scrap of food stopped short. His face held an expression that turned into a sneer.

'Is he your son, perhaps?' he murmured, directed at Trygg. He casually tossed the piece of meat back, landing at Marcus's feet.

'The question is rather, who is the mother, Trygg or the Jarl himself?' one of the berserk's companions quipped.

The boat fell quiet. Trygg raised his eyebrows, turning his head slowly to face the two insolent warriors.

'You squeal like piglets, and you're not half as clever. Can't you pretend to be men and speak up about what's bothering you?'

The man who picked up Marcus's dried meat, of stocky build with short dark hair and a long beard, glared at Trygg.

'You know well that the Jarl cheated us. He's soft as a bog in spring!'

'Careful now, berserk, before you say something that cannot be unsaid,' Trygg cautioned, as he threw a solemn glance at Geir Galne.

Geir Galne, the leader of the berserks, leaned back languidly as if looking forward to the outcome of this simmering spectacle. He was tall and slender, with thinning unkempt hair, more grey than brown. Bulging eyes made it uncomfortable for anyone to meet his gaze. The narrow pointed faced, racked with battle scars was blank and unreadable.

Trygg's gaze returned to rest upon the two warriors.

'You both got your share of the loot. It's neither mine nor the Jarl's fault that you killed the women before you could present them to the Jarl. Two thralls offer far greater value than what little silver we could wring from this hole of a village.'

'We were in battle! The two bitches kicked and clawed! Should we not have defended ourselves?'

Trygg chuckled. 'Poor boy! Did the wench scratch you?' he replied, as if he were comforting a child who had scraped his knee.

The second warrior rose abruptly. He was a bigger man with a long, sharp scar that snaked from temple to jaw.

'We were cheated from our fair share of the loot!'

'Sit down, dimwit!' Magnus Trygg raised his voice.

Every movement and conversation on board stopped. Even the weather had calmed as if the sea god Njord himself decided to pause and watch the exchange.

The battle-marked berserk did not sit down. Instead, his hand found and closed around the shaft of an axe propped against a ship chest. The smaller berserk stooped and picked up his spear that rested near his feet. Trygg rose, advanced two steps and in one swift motion, drew his sword. The veteran, who had seemed burdened by age earlier in the day, showed no signs of weakness now. Fighting alone against two opponents was ever a dangerous exercise, especially from someone without a shield. The experienced warrior positioned himself with the mast on his left, forcing the larger berserk to move around on either side if he wanted to swing his axe freely against his target.

Trygg could not advance on the berserks without losing what little protection the mast provided. He smiled and challenged the spear-wielding opponent.

'Come on, wench, or are you afraid I'll scratch you?'

The warrior lunged at the bait like a starved catfish. He took a quick step forward and stabbed at Trygg.

Without the shield, Trygg's left hand was free. He sidestepped and grabbed the spear, passing a hand's breadth from his flank. He jerked it towards him, extending the attacker's momentum forward. It was too quick; the unbalanced berserk failed to comprehend that he was now faced with a fatal choice – release the spear or die.

He held on to the spear.

Trygg slashed his neck, severing the thick vein, as the berserk plunged forward, the once brutish opponent now quiet.

No longer outnumbered, Trygg was still perilously exposed. The massive, scarred warrior had moved around the mast and was in position to swing his axe. The ship's mast, now on his right side, denied Trygg full use of his sword arm. Worse, his sword was still wedged in the neck of the now lifeless berserk, a dead weight slumped between the chests.

The bigger of the two, the berserk now seized the opportunity to lunge with his axe, in a full, deadly arc against Trygg's unprotected left. Trygg was the quicker, and kicked hard against his foe's stomach. The axe-wielder lost his footing and stumbled, the blade just slicing the air in front of Trygg's chest. The warrior fell on his back and landed in Ulv's lap. Keeping his eyes on Trygg, he struggled to regain his footing. Ulv gave him a firm push, his hand brushing against something on the man's belt.

Now, Trygg held the upper hand. He recovered his sword and moved in on the berserk. The burly warrior snorted in protest and charged. He caught Trygg's sword arm with his left hand, changed his grip on the axe and grabbed it by the shaft just below the blade. In this position, he did not need much space to swing it against the veteran's face. Trygg anticipated the move and locked his opponent's wrist with his free left hand.

The two men were now locked in a battle of will and strength. Neither seemed to gain leverage over the other. They shuffled around each other, breathing heavily, eyes fixed. In unison, they let go of each other's wrists, grabbed their knives and jabbed. Their timing so perfectly coordinated, it seemed almost rehearsed.

The berserk stared wide-eyed at Magnus Trygg. His hand frantically patting around at his belt, searching his knife. He glanced down only to see Trygg's knife, now driven into his gut up to the hilt. Lifting his gaze again, dumbfounded, before he slumped on to the deck, his bewildered eyes resting on Ulv as he drew his last breath.

Ulv glanced around. As the crew's attention was on the expiring berserk, he pulled the knife out of his sleeve and laid it on the deck in a discreet motion.

Meanwhile, Magnus Trygg wiped his knife clean on the dead man's cloak and sheathed it back on his belt. He shook his head and exhaled through pursed lips while looking down at the man he had just killed. His gaze shifted to Geir Galne, who shrugged and continued chewing as if nothing had happened.

Chapter 7: Thralls

Marcus reached out and picked up the meat that had cost the two men their lives. This particular morsel tasted better than the ones he had eaten before. While he ate, he glanced at the young Northman who unwittingly held the key to his destiny; their fates were now intertwined.

So young and slight was he, smaller than all the others. He seemed just as frightened as Marcus himself, the morning they met in the cellar. Still, since their opportune meeting, he had conquered his fears and challenged a giant of a man to a duel and won. Now, he had saved the life of this man, Magnus Trygg, the only Viking who had shown any semblance of kindness. His father often said that a brave man is no less afraid than others, but finds the courage to do what he has to when faced with fear.

His father would have liked Ulv if they had met.

Shouts and cheers woke Marcus from his daze. It took him some time to read the situation and understand what was happening. He got to his feet and looked in the same direction as the crew. It felt like a massive blow, a pit in his stomach. A third ship had appeared and now trailed behind the other two that left the beach on their course north. It was apparent from the cheers and ruckus among the crew that the ship was party to their conquest. Marcus swayed, leaned over the railing and vomited the thin rye porridge and the costly strip of meat he had just eaten.

Of course, Marcus knew what happened when the heathens raided monasteries or other villages but had hoped it would not occur in Wucestre. The Vikings attacked at daybreak, robbing their victims the time to organise resistance or plan their escape. In addition, they sent a unit of warriors, whose task was to cut off those who tried to flee. Ensuring these could be taken as slaves. Any goods that they sought to hurry away to hidden caches were added to the spoils of the raid.

Marcus could not see who or what was in the third boat, but he assumed the worst, that it was the same group of townspeople he had passed by when he ran back home to join his father in the defence. His head pounded with the thought of Julia on that ship, and he found little comfort in the hope that she managed to get away safely. Marcus felt sick again.

'Thralls?' Marcus asked.

He wiped his mouth and looked at Ulv. The third ship had come close enough for the crews to shout to each other. Marcus would like to ask more, but he could not find the right words in the language of the Northmen. Ulv nodded without looking at him.

'Many?'

'Nineteen,' Ulv answered.

Marcus tallied frantically in his head.

The wife of the blacksmith and their three children, the baker's wife and their son Nick, the two young daughters of the tailor …

Counting on his fingers as he listed them mentally.

Thirteen. Fourteen with Julia. He had to count to nineteen without including Julia! Abbi? Had he seen her, or her siblings? She would probably have been there. There were others he could not recall. Again, fourteen, fifteen, sixteen.

Over and over, he counted. He recalled the familiar faces he had met on his way back to the village after bidding Julia farewell, but to no avail. His head hurt and throbbed. He could not be sure how many they were. There was only one way to learn if they had taken her, he had to get a look on that third ship.

Marcus abandoned his helpless counting, closed his eyes and clasped his hands together. It felt strange to him as if his fingers did not fit with his other hand.

Dear God, save Julia from the Vikings' claws. Anything, just let Julia go.

Chapter 8: Sanday

Ulv stood in the bow and admired the lush islands. For two days, they had sailed with the land of the Picts on their port side. Now, they had reached Orkneyjar, which the Northmen for decades had used as an advanced base for trade and raids. Several farms with stone buildings appeared as they navigated between the small islands covered by hills and steep cliffs. Seabirds flocked around small fishing boats, and sheep grazed the fields.

They followed the Jarl's ship along the coast of one of the largest and northernmost islands. Ulv regarded the many beaches of the isle Magnus Trygg had called Sanday, where they would rest and resupply.

The ships glided into a sheltered bay where two dozen similar vessels were hauled all the way up to the shore. Two longships were arranged keel-up on stone walls, serving as roofs for longhouses in the makeshift harbour. In addition to the houses, a score of tents were scattered above the beach.

On the port side, a peninsula connected with the rest of the island via a narrow stretch of grassland. The surrounding coastline consisted of rocks and small cliffs. At the highest point stood an ancient-looking stone tower, missing the roof and parts of its walls. Stone mounds protruded above the grass. Ulv assumed them to be old burial sites.

The Northmen's ships had broad hulls that lay high in the water, allowing them to sail up shallow bays and rivers. The oarsmen rowed until the keel scraped against the sand. Then, a dozen of them jumped overboard and pulled the vessel further up the beach. Soon, the jubilant crew wobbled towards the longhouses on unsteady legs.

Ulv shrugged, looked over at Marcus and nodded towards the camp. Ulv was ashore before he discovered that his new thrall lingered behind, stretching his neck to look at the other two ships.

'The prisoners are chained on board,' Ulv replied, to the question that had not been uttered. 'I guess they will be kept there until the Jarl has decided where to sell them.'

'And I?' Marcus asked.

'I don't know. I've never had a thrall before,' Ulv said.

Marcus's face radiated apprehension as he followed his new master towards the bustling camp. Ulv quickly calculated that there were far more people than there was room for. The men were busy preparing the ships for the next voyage. Provisions and equipment were loaded. Some repaired weapons and armour. Others trained in the small battle formations. Women and children made ropes and mended sails.

Ulv overheard some crewmembers talking excitedly about the prospects of the island. The population was expanding at home, and access to arable land was limited. Here, there was land for farming and pasture for cattle. Some considered the Orkneyjar an opportunity for a better life, and brought their families across the North Sea.

Ulv and Marcus followed the road up from the beach towards a nearby farm. At a crossroads, where a smaller path led out towards the tower on the peninsula, they encountered Sigurd Jarl and two of his housecarls.

The Jarl stopped and regarded Ulv as if he discovered a notch in his favourite sword. He was silent for a moment, scratching his grey-speckled beard.

'I promised you a safe journey home. We can still get you there, but not right now. You'll have to wait here until we get back.'

The Jarl looked questioningly at Ulv. When there was no answer, he continued. 'Or you can sail with the slaves to Hedeby, and find a ship home from there.'

'Where are you going?' asked Ulv, hesitantly.

Sigurd Jarl grinned. 'We will join Torgils's fleet raiding the Green Isle!'

Ulv did not share the Jarl's enthusiasm. He had clung to his hope of returning home as a free man. The voyage had been a mistake, and he felt utterly out of place on this island of warriors and farmers. Ulv was quite sure he was neither. He strived to look cold and determined as he nodded to the Jarl.

'We shall wait here.'

Ulv and Marcus walked in silence through a field of barley. As befits a thrall, Marcus walked a few steps behind his new master. Ulv found the arrangement strange and uncomfortable. He pointed to a part of the field where they grew a different crop.

'Wheat?' Ulv asked over his shoulder.

'Yes.'

The young thrall seemed to understand most of what was said, when spoken slowly. On the few occasions Marcus spoke, he used few words. It did not sound right, but it was close enough to understand what he meant. If given more time to prepare, he would use more words, with fewer mistakes. Ulv did not know why Marcus was familiar with the Norse language, or whether this was common among his people. He decided to ask about it when they got home.

The farmstead was located on a small hill. Four longhouses formed a square with an open area in the middle. Several smaller buildings were scattered around, including a bathhouse similar to those Ulv was used to from home. There was smoke from a stone building that looked like a smithy.

Outside the smithy, three men making arrows caught Ulv's attention. A batch of arrowheads were longer and narrower than the regular ones. Ulv stooped and picked up a handful.

'Why are they so narrow?' he asked.

'They bore deeper through thick skin,' the eldest of the fletchers said, 'and strong armour'.

'This is outstanding work,' Ulv said, and returned some of the arrowheads to the bowl. The rest found their way to a small fold under his sleeve. He wanted to examine them later. Ulv rose to leave, nodded briefly to the men and glanced at Marcus. If the thrall noticed the sleight-of-hand, he did not mention it as they left the farm and sauntered back towards the ships.

'Look, there goes the whelp with his favourite bitch.'

Ulv looked over his shoulder to see Kjetil Korte and three companions approach with long strides. His stomach tightened as he turned to face them. Kjetil seemed extraordinarily cheerful. A bad omen. Ulv tried to keep his composure while his eyes searched for the Jarl. He found some of Torgils's warriors nearby, but none of Sigurd Jarl's men.

'There's no one who can help you now, whelp! You have no friends here, either!' Kjetil said, louder than necessary.

Ulv did not reply.

'You fight like a cowardly rat!' Kjetil roared for everyone to hear.

The brute was only a few steps away when Ulv realised what was going on. If Kjetil attacked him, he would dishonour Sigurd Jarl's promise. But he could, of course, defend himself if Ulv threw the first punch.

A confident smile spread on Ulv's face. He did not intend to fight this giant again, no matter how much bile he coughed up.

'Are you trying to get your revenge by boring me to death?'

Ulv could not help but grin when he turned to resume his walk.

Kjetil put a massive paw on Ulv's shoulder and yanked him around. His cheerful mood was gone. The muscles of his jaw were tight, the nostrils flared. Bushy eyebrows were pulled down towards the bridge of the nose.

'You stole my loot!' he hissed through clenched teeth.

Ulv froze. *No, no, no, do not tell that story while Marcus is listening!*

The reaction reinforced Kjetil's aggression.

'You stole him from me, the old man with—'

Ulv exploded into motion. He spun around as he bent down and sent his right foot in a wide arc. Kjetil could not react before Ulv's foot hit him hard in the ankle. The giant's right foot slid on the grass and connected with his left. He fell heavily. Down, but not out.

Ulv hesitated for a moment. He had to stop Kjetil before Marcus could make sense of his tale. *But how?*

The slight indecision cost Ulv dearly. Roaring, Kjetil reached for Ulv's leg and grabbed the fabric of his trousers. Ulv anticipated his next move. To avoid falling on his back when Kjetil pulled, Ulv jumped towards him and slammed his right knee in the big red face of the giant.

But Kjetil was no ordinary man. He seized the boy and writhed to get on top of him. Ulv realised that this was not going to go his way. Firmly in the grip of Kjetil's massive fists, he could no longer rely on his quickness and agility to keep out of harm's way. His desperate efforts at breaking free were utterly futile.

Soon, the giant warrior sat on his chest and placed his heavy knees on Ulv's upper arms to pin him to the ground. Snarling, Kjetil clasped his hands around his neck. *Two hands*, Ulv thought, *seem excessive.*

Ulv managed to wriggle one hand free and got hold of one of the fingers around his neck. He felt something hard and cold against his fingertips, and pulled. It was too late. He could not summon the strength to fight this monster, to break free or even to survive.

In his last moments, Ulv studied Kjetil's red face. His expression was a mixture of pain, anger and satisfaction. His body weakened as his life force waned, and he could not see clearly. The red face above him was a red surface, without contours. A blood-red sun. *After sunset comes the black night*, was the last, unfocused thought that went through Ulv's head.

Chapter 9: Laughter

Marcus started laughing, so loud that he caught the attention of the Northmen. Shaking his head, he turned towards the beach camp, still laughing. He was not surprised when a strong fist grabbed hold of his arm.

'Hey, bitch! Where do you think you are going?'

Kjetil towered over him. His face threatened to burst with rage. He turned Marcus around with a jerk, clasped his huge fists around his upper arms and lifted him off the ground. Kjetil roared something, too fast and indistinct for Marcus to understand. Based on the grimaces and the amount of saliva that came with it, he was displeased.

Marcus suppressed an impulse to kick. According to their custom, the heathen would have every right to kill a slave who attacked him. Instead, he forced himself to hang like a sack, without resisting.

'What are you laughing at, thrall?'

Marcus smiled again and met Kjetil's gaze.

'Northman kills Northman. You kill the boy. The Jarl kills you.'

They locked eyes. The other warriors were silent. Kjetil began to breathe more calmly, and the red colour faded. As his eyes narrowed, he shifted his grip on Marcus and launched him through the air. Marcus flew several man-lengths before he thumped to the rocky ground.

Chapter 10: Debt

Ulv awoke to voices in the distance, surprised to be alive. His neck ached as if it had been squeezed flat. Through blurred eyes, he saw several figures towering over him, but he could not make out who they were. The figures disappeared. Ulv tightened his hand around the small metal object he had gotten hold of during the fight with Kjetil.

Eventually, he managed to breathe without hissing, and his vision became sharper. As the men's laughter faded, he turned his head carefully and saw Marcus lying motionless on his back two dozen steps away. Ulv crawled on his hands and knees and found Marcus looking up at the clouds with a thoughtful expression, and bleeding from a cut under the eye.

'Are you injured?' asked Ulv.

Marcus raised an eyebrow in response. He turned to Ulv and asked:

'Who was the old man you killed?'

Ulv rose to his knees. He stretched his neck, turned his head from side to side and used his fingers to check if he was bleeding anywhere. There was no blood. He glanced up at the sky and sighed.

'A man charged me as I ran between the buildings. He struck with his sword, I stabbed with the knife. He missed, I hit. It was over in the blink of an eye.' Ulv demonstrated by snapping with both hands, almost simultaneously. He spoke more slowly than usual, so Marcus would have a chance to understand what he said.

'Who was he?'

'I did not have time to ask.'

Marcus's eyes narrowed. 'What did he look like?'

'Much like you. Only bigger and older,' replied Ulv, forcing himself to meet Marcus's gaze.

The man he killed had the same brown eyes as Marcus. He had known it from the first time he saw the boy in the cellar under the burning house. Ulv regarded Marcus without speaking and observed how his face changed expression several times. His brow wrinkled over angry eyes. His jaw tightened.

'The big man should kill you,' Marcus said as he stood.

Ulv glanced up at him. 'Do you mean that Kjetil tried to kill me, or that you want him to kill me?'

'Yes!' Marcus replied, turning his back on Ulv and walking towards the ships.

Ulv got to his feet and followed his thrall, whose father he had killed with a knife stab to the stomach. He hid away the ring. It did not seem like the right moment to give to Marcus.

Ulv stayed a few steps behind as they walked.

'What should I do then?' asked Ulv to his back in front of him.

'Stay home!'

'I am sorry!' Ulv said, and stopped.

Marcus also halted, and turned halfway towards Ulv.

'What is "sorry"?'

'It means I'm sad,' Ulv replied, and immediately regretted it.

'You're sad,' Marcus repeated.

This really did not go well.

'How can I repair the damage?'

'The damage?'

'Yes, because I killed your father.'

'Is it damage?'

'Not damage,' Ulv replied, resigned. It was not easy to talk about something so complicated with someone who did not understand the meaning of his words, 'but damage to you. I've destroyed something that was yours. I'm in debt to you.'

'Debt?' Marcus said. He frowned and shook his head. 'Did you buy my father from me?'

'No, I did not buy your father. But I'm indebted to you for causing your father's death. Everyone has their price, and once that price is paid, the debt is settled.'

'How much is your debt, then?'

'Not much. Nothing, I think.'

'Why not?'

'Your father was a thrall. You're also a thrall. There is no man-fine for killing a thrall.'

'He was a merchant!'

'Your father lost the fight, and now he is dead. Alive, he would have been a thrall. But he was old, and his value would be low.'

Marcus grimaced, closed his eyes and pinched the bridge of his nose.

'A thrall for a thrall?' he asked after a while.

Ulv studied the dark-haired boy, a year or two younger than himself. He could understand his anger, but had no idea where he was going with this.

'What do you mean?'

'Your debt to me.' Marcus continued as he met Ulv's gaze. 'Your debt to me is one thrall? True?'

Ulv nodded slowly, still at a loss.

'Fine. Then you give me one thrall,' Marcus said with a determined look.

Ulv sighed, and spoke very slowly when he answered.

'You are a thrall. You can't own a thrall. I still do not understand what you mean.'

'Do you agree? Your debt? Thrall for thrall?'

'Yes, it seems about right …' Ulv did not want to respond, but Marcus was insistent.

'Agree?' Marcus's voice rose higher, a twinkle in his eyes.

'I agree.' Ulv conceded to the simple logic.

Ulv felt his conscience gnaw, but was not quite sure why. It happened in battle, and Marcus's father held his sword ready to strike. The old man died fighting. It was the most honourable fate, and more than any old merchant could hope for. Maybe he would never get the same chance again? It was common sense, but still, it did not feel right.

Marcus fixed Ulv's eyes with a resolute expression.

'I have a sister.' He stabbed his finger once at Ulv's chest. 'She is your debt to me.' His eyes narrowed, and he pushed harder. 'Thrall for thrall.'

Chapter 11: News

At sundown, Ulv went to look for Julia on the ship that carried the captives. A thrall for a thrall. How had he ended up in such a situation? He had promised a thrall that he would find his sister. Find the sister, yes. And then? What would he do if he located her? He did not have the means to buy her, even if the Jarl was willing to sell. The alternative was to rescue her, steal a ship and sail to a distant island where the three of them could live in peace and prosperity. Ulv shook his head as he trudged across the grass.

Flickering lights lit up the campsites of those who were not important enough to sleep under a roof. Song and laughter sounded from all sides. A figure approached Ulv, his silhouette outlined by the bonfires. It was Geir Galne, strolling with a mug in his hand and a crooked grin on his gaunt face. A straw stuck out from the left corner of his mouth.

He stopped in front of Ulv, took a sip of the mug and spoke in a hoarse voice. 'Well, hello there, pup! Are you sniffing around all alone?'

Ulv did not doubt this man was dangerous. His calm demeanour, the devious smile and the balanced stance only made Ulv more restless. At ease, yet ready for anything. The name Galne was Norse for madman, and only added to his notoriety. Something about him did not seem right.

Ulv did not come up with any clever retorts, so he simply said 'Geir' and nodded.

Galne moved the straw to the other corner of his mouth.

'You know, a tiny puppy shouldn't be barking so much.'

Ulv did not answer. What should he say?

Galne took a step closer and continued: 'At least not when there are wolves around that do not like the sound of small dogs whining. And in that picture, you're not a wolf, Ulv. Do you understand?'

'Are you the wolf?' asked Ulv, genuinely curious.

'Ha ha, in this tale I'm one of the wolves. A small wolf, albeit with sharp teeth and an unpredictable temper, but there are many wolves here.'

The bulging, blue eyes studied Ulv's face. The berserk stepped so close that Ulv smelled the beer on his breath.

'And there's a new wolf here now. The biggest wolf you've ever seen. So be careful, Ulv. Just a friendly warning from a small wolf to an even smaller one …'

Galne's mouth pulled up in a half-smile as if he was thoroughly pleased with his eloquence.

Ulv opened his mouth to speak. No words came to mind, so he closed it again.

Geir Galne, apparently satisfied with the conversation, turned and strolled back towards the camp while singing loudly about a 'black goddess'. Ulv did not know if Galne delivered a warning or a threat, or the ramblings of a madman. Possibly a bit of everything all at once.

Ulv returned to his task of ascertaining whether Marcus's sister was among the captives on the third ship. An investigation better performed in secrecy he decided, and chose a route that avoided light sources and people. If he could sneak on board the vessel, identify Julia, and return without being seen, the risks would be minimal. If, on the other hand, someone spotted him and realised he was somewhere he should not be, he might never see another dawn. He would rather not talk to anyone this night.

As Ulv approached the ship, he pulled up the hood of the cloak and stepped quickly over the wet sand. He slowed down when he reached the water's edge and waded until he could grab the boards and climb up.

Under some canvas at the stern, a miserable assembly of captives were embracing each other for warmth and comfort. Ulv was just about close enough to discern their faces when he heard a dark voice from behind.

'Hey! What do you want?'

Ulv turned to see a warrior with a spear in his hand climbing on board the same place he had done just before.

'I'm looking for a girl for the Jarl,' Ulv replied, turning to the thralls again.

'The Jarl? Torgils's already got two girls. How many does he need?'

'One more, it seems,' Ulv replied. 'Do you have a problem with that?'

Ulv gave the man a challenging look before he turned back to the thralls. 'What do the other two look like?'

The warrior pulled his hand down the braid in his light beard.

'Look like? Well, they look … Why are you asking about that?'

Ulv sighed in exasperation.

'Do I have to explain everything to you? Can't you just answer? If the two girls are alike, then I know he prefers a particular type. Were they different, I know he prefers variety. So, can you please tell me what the girls look like?'

Ulv's courage grew as the warrior in front of him seemed more and more hesitant.

'Varia …?'

'That they are different!'

'Eh, they are both dark-haired, I mean. Young. Thin. I do not remember much more. I can ask some of the other guys …'

'No, thank you. That won't be necessary,' Ulv interrupted. He did not trust his improvised ruse to work on another guard. 'I have what I need,' he said, turning to the thralls, studying them closely.

None of the young girls on board matched the description Marcus had given him. Both relieved and disappointed, Ulv did not look forward to telling Marcus that two dark-haired girls had been gifted to Torgils. Ulv stepped past the guard and climbed down from the ship.

'Shouldn't you be taking a girl with you?' the Viking asked after him.

'No, I did not find what I was looking for,' Ulv replied over his shoulder.

'Did you find her?' Marcus asked eagerly, as Ulv approached the campfire.

'I have good news and bad news,' Ulv replied calmly. 'What do you want first?'

'Tell me!'

Ulv suppressed his impulse to answer that the girls were too pretty to be related to Marcus. 'I did not find her. But the guard told me that two girls had been brought to Torgils. He gave a description that fitted Julia. '

'What was good news?' Marcus asked with a raised eyebrow.

Ulv shrugged. 'Well, I could have had much worse news.'

Marcus punched the ground in despair. Whether by anger, or because he simply did not understand, Ulv could not tell.

'Torgils?'

Ulv got the impression that Marcus thought he should have done more to find Julia. 'We can try to learn more tomorrow.' He stretched out his hands towards the fire.

'Tomorrow?' Marcus sounded troubled. 'What will happen to her tonight?'

'Something unpleasant, I'm afraid. But there is nothing we can do for your sister now. I can't just enter Torgils's house and command him to hand over his thralls.'

Marcus stared at Ulv, but did not answer.

Ulv stared into the flames for some time before he spoke.

'Torgils's camp is out there,' Ulv pointed towards the peninsula. 'His housecarls guard the path. I doubt they will let us pass, with or without the girls.'

Marcus did not reply, but Ulv felt his gaze bore into him.

Chapter 12: Blot

'I think I know who we can ask,' Ulv said the next morning. 'Geir Galne loves to talk.'

'Fine,' Marcus replied.

Ulv glanced at Marcus, but could not tell what lay behind the short answer. He shrugged and set off.

They found Galne sleeping on his back in front of a tent above the beach. A straw hung from the corner of his mouth. Ulv hesitated, contemplating the wisdom in waking him up.

'What brings the little puppy, and the even smaller puppy, to my little castle?' asked Galne, without opening his eyes.

'I was wondering if a big wolf like you had been visiting the old tower and met the even bigger wolf out there?' Ulv replied, hoping to get goodwill from the berserk by continuing the jargon from the night before.

Marcus glanced from Ulv to Galne, and back to Ulv, with a frown. Ulv ignored him, concentrating on Galne.

'Yes, I have seen the black warg and his pack,' Galne replied. He opened one eye to look at Ulv. 'What has that got to do with the little puppy?'

'The little puppy does not know what's going on here,' Ulv replied.

'No, it's something that little puppies should not put their snouts in.'

Galne closed his eyes again.

Ulv turned to Marcus and shrugged apologetically.

'We will set out on a raid in two days. And tomorrow night there will be a feast.' Galne moved the straw to the other corner of his mouth. 'The black wolf has a bit of a bitch, too. Her name is Aud, and she can speak with the gods. She is as deadly as she is attractive, and she will come along for the journey. Her black heart is set on giving every man and woman on the Green Isle the choice between sacrificing to Odin, or being sacrificed themselves. She is the one who does not want stray dogs sniffing around on the headland. That's why they have guard dogs that bite any uninvited visitor.'

Galne fell quiet again. A moment later, he snored. Ulv shrugged and started walking away.

'What did he say?' Marcus asked as he caught up with him.

'Not much, really. Tomorrow, we honour the gods. The day after the feast, we embark. And it will be difficult to get out there.'

Ulv shifted his gaze to the headland and a group of five seasoned warriors approaching. Their demeanour set them apart from the band of Vikings Ulv had sailed with. Veterans all, radiating authority. They moved with confidence, apparently unaffected by the heavy equipment. Two walked with their thumb tucked inside their belt, near the handle of sword or axe. Calm and relaxed, but nonetheless alert. They were well equipped, with padded armour and decorated sword hilts. Several wore braids in their hair and beards, fastened with silver rings and jewellery.

'What happens at a feast?' Marcus asked, turning to Ulv.

'The feast? Well, there will be eating and drinking, of course. Much eating, and even more drinking,' Ulv replied. 'And maybe a blot, as we're about to depart on a raid.'

'Blot?'

'Yes, blot. Sacrifice,' Ulv replied. Seeing Marcus's questioning expression, he added, 'To the gods.'

'Sacrifice? Humans? Thralls? Girls?' Marcus reddened and waved his arms in exasperation.

Ulv had not thought of that. He was about to reply that it was unlikely, but Aud had a reputation for being overly zealous in her service to the gods. Rumours told she did things no other *volve* would do. Terrible things. Maybe that was why Torgils sent for the two thralls?

'I don't know,' he replied hesitantly, 'I do not think so.'

Marcus shook his head and turned away.

*

In the evening, the camp bustled with activity. The mood was rising, and men and women were joking and laughing as they were making preparations for the feast. Sheep and chickens were brought from the farm, in addition to great quantities of mead and beer. Benches and tables were carried and arranged outside the two longhouses. Makeshift fireplaces for preparing large amounts of food were built and lit.

Ulv and Marcus kept an eye on the people coming and going. After the confrontation with Kjetil, Ulv was unsure about his standing among the crew. He had been largely overlooked by Sigurd's men, and only exchanged a few words and trivialities with others.

Marcus was still seething. Despite their inquiries, they had not learned anything about the two thralls. In silence, they watched as Northmen and Danes assembled between the longhouses, finding seats by the tables or standing in small groups. Soon, they were all drinking heartily, and shouts, laughs and fistfights erupted all around.

By sunset, the area in front of one of the longhouses was cleared. Sigurd Jarl and a handful of his housecarls disappeared into the house, talking and laughing as they went. A tall bench and several buckets and troughs were placed outside, and dozens of torches were lit. When the area bathed in the soft, orange light from fires and the last rays from the setting sun, the crowd cheered as a slender man wielding a massive sword sauntered into the square. He wore a long apron over his clothes, and from his broad leather belt hung a collection of knives and axes of various sizes.

'The butcher,' muttered Ulv.

Again, cheers rose around them. Two figures appeared, a man and a woman. No doubt Torgils and his volve and mistress, Aud. The dark-haired warlord wore polished chain mail armour, tall leather shoes, several rings and a silver necklace with a Tor's hammer pendant. The hilt of the sword richly decorated. Under his right arm, he carried an ornate helmet.

Aud had long blonde hair with a reddish sheen. A massive silver torc hung over a long green dress of thin and light fabric. On her head, she wore a narrow band of braided silver. Torchlight reflected from rings on both hands.

The couple arrived at the longhouse and turned towards the crowd. Torgils demanded silence by lifting his arms, and the men duly obeyed. He spoke in a deep and clear voice.

'Tomorrow we depart for the Green Isle!'

Torgils waited until the ensuing cheers subsided.

'This will be the boldest raid the world has ever seen. We sail with two dozen ships and hundreds of warriors!'

The audience roared with approval. Torgils held up a hand again.

'Tonight, we feast! But first …'

Torgils withdrew a few steps.

Aud stepped forward, shouting in a loud and shrill voice:

'Let the blot begin!'

Ulv glanced at Marcus who stood pale and wide-eyed by his side. He stared at the opening between the longhouses where Torgils and Aud had entered the square. Ulv followed his gaze and saw men carrying lambs or chickens, others pulling sheep and cows, even a horse. Thus far, there were no thrall women to be seen. Marcus stretched his neck to better see what was happening.

Aud spoke again:

'Let the *soa* begin!'

The butcher seized a hen, chopped off its head and passed it on to a man who turned it upside down and drained its blood into a bucket. Then he picked up another unfortunate bird and repeated the ritual. Again and again, until the butcher dropped one of the beheaded chickens on the ground.

Promptly, it darted straight through the crowd, bringing the jubilation to new heights.

Larger animals were slaughtered, and soon buckets and troughs were filled with warm blood. Aud made some signs and gestures over the vessels and uttered a series of unintelligible words. Then, she and Torgils both grabbed brushes and a bucket and started splashing blood on the longhouse door and walls.

Chapter 13: Blood

More men arrived, and in the commotion, it soon became impossible for Marcus to see if more victims were brought forward.

He wondered what he would do if Julia was brought in front of this man. It was pointless to expect any help. Even though Ulv promised to help him find his sister, he would not sacrifice his life in the process. Understandable really, but Marcus could not help being annoyed that Ulv did not care more. Marcus did not harbour much expectation for the assistance the young Viking would give. Nevertheless, Ulv was the closest Marcus had to a friend at the moment, and he had at least expressed a desire to help.

Marcus wanted to leave. If Julia was brought forth, he would not be able to do anything anyway. Cold but sweating all the same, he realised he could not leave. There was only one thing to do, he had to get closer. Had to see. He pulled at Ulv's arm, and together they moved towards the butcher. Marcus's gaze fell on Aud and Torgils.

Marcus despised them for strutting around like king and queen. He despised them for taking Julia as a slave.

And he hated them because they were going to sacrifice her.

Marcus and Ulv bent down and pushed sideways between the broad-shouldered men who blocked the view. At the front, the area was packed with people, and they could not get further. Hearing Aud's voice right in front of him, but seeing nothing, Marcus stretched to look around, bent down to look between, and he jumped to look over. To no avail.

Suddenly strong hands took hold of his waist and hoisted him into the air.

'The boy wants blood!'

'What?' Marcus tried to turn and see who held him. At the same time, something wet and hot slapped his face. It stung his eyes and ran down his cheeks. Marcus rubbed his eyes, trying to see what was going on. Aud stood in front of him with a bucket and brush and flung blood. The heathens surrounding him rejoiced.

Marcus wriggled and twisted until he was down on the ground again. He ploughed his way out of the crowd, away from the mob, the animals and the blood. Away from the people, all these terrible people. He stumbled on and clawed at his face trying to get the blood out of his eyes.

Chapter 14: Departure

Ulv registered that Marcus withdrew, but he remained with the other Vikings, fascinated by the scenes that unfolded. The mead was now blessed and passed around for the toasts. First came Odin's toast, with shouts of victory and power to Torgils. Afterwards, they performed Njord's toast with requests for safe travel and good fortunes for ships and crew. They drank to Freyr, too, for peace and a good year. As the crowd started to dissolve, they kept going in smaller groups. There were toasts for Brage, for their relatives and for those who had passed away – the toast of minne. Some of Sigurd's men emptied their mugs for Torvald, the only man who had not survived the attack on the village.

Soon, the women brought food to the tables, and thus began the third and final part of the blot.

Ulv waited to have some food, and looked forward to finally being able to share some good news with Marcus. He found his thrall friend sitting by a rock behind one of the longhouses, staring into the dark night and looking utterly miserable. The blood smears on his face created a stark contrast to the pale skin underneath. In his attempts at wiping his tears, he painted dark circles around his eyes.

Ulv hurriedly shared the good news. 'Julia is safe!'

Marcus turned his head towards him, and Ulv took the opportunity to provide more detailed information. 'The blot is over, and they sacrificed no one. The thralls are safe, for now.'

Marcus met his gaze for a moment. He nodded, but turned away and stared into the darkness again.

Ulv sat down next to him, placed a bowl of meat between them and ate a piece of scorched chicken.

*

The next morning, Ulv went out early to find a way to the headland where Torgils lived with Aud and his housecarls. It was strangely quiet, as though he was the only one realising it was morning. The guard was half asleep, and Ulv reached the cape without being stopped. Near the Pictish stone tower in the heart of Torgils's camp, a warrior stopped him. He moved gingerly, his face and eyes revealed that he had participated wholeheartedly in the feast the night before.

'What do you want, boy?'

'Eh, no, I'm just, I'm looking for a thrall I caught. In Northumbria,' Ulv replied, opting for a half-truth for lack of better alternatives.

'Here, you will only find Torgils's thralls. Soon, you will find nobody. Everyone's leaving today. Get out of here, you'll just be in the way.'

Ulv left happy, pleased to finally discover useful information. He returned to the camp where Marcus waited impatiently.

'Torgils brings everybody along for the raid,' Ulv greeted the Northumbrian.

'Did you see Julia?' Marcus asked with a concerned look.

'No, I did not get close enough before I was stopped by a warrior. He rejected me, but not before saying that everybody would leave. The thralls too.' This time, Ulv spoke slowly to give Marcus the chance to understand.

'We must join the raid!' Marcus answered resolutely, grabbed his blanket and started walking towards the ships.

'This is not your decision to make, thrall,' Ulv whispered while he rolled up his blanket.

Marcus would follow Torgils through Niflheim if he thought he had any chance of finding his sister. The problem was that Ulv could not see a future for himself as an outcast on the Orkneyjar or in Hedeby. Therefore, he accepted his thrall's decision, picked up what little equipment he had at the small campsite, and caught up with Marcus before he reached the shore.

'Where are you going?' Kjetil Korte called for them.

'Raid!' Marcus said before Ulv could come up with a sensible reply.

'Ha ha, the puny puppy and his thrall bitch going on a raid? What are you going to do there? You are useless! No, you have not earned the right to join us. Go away!'

Magnus Trygg came walking towards them. He looked at Kjetil and said:

'I'm pleased to see that you care for the boys, Kjetil. They should stay here, safe from harm, until we return. On raids, they would be in constant danger and it would be close to impossible to keep them safe.'

Magnus patiently held Kjetil's gaze, until the brute's expression changed from anger to vicious glee.

'Of course you boys can join the raid! We don't want you to rot here while we are away!' Kjetil said, grinning.

Magnus Trygg nodded to Ulv. 'Find a place in my ship. We sail at midday.'

Chapter 15: Pain

Julia awoke to a wave of pain shooting through her body. Followed by another wave, and another. She opened her eyes and tried to understand where she was, and what hurt so much. The ground above her moved like a boat in a storm. *Above?* With her right hand, she hugged her broken left arm to her chest. Still, it stung and pounded with every step. *Step? Whose steps?* She looked down at wet shoes. There was something familiar about them. The river, the dog, the ships.

Julia hung upside down over the shoulder of a man who walked quickly through the rugged terrain. His wet pants clung to his legs as he walked, and she could see glimpses of hairy legs above his leather shoes as he strode.

Her fingers found the small dagger attached to her forearm. Carefully, she lifted her arm to her mouth, and with her teeth she loosened the leather strap that held the knife in place. She clenched her teeth over the sheath, and drew the knife with her right hand. Biting hard on the scabbard in her mouth prevented her from screaming as her broken arm swung against the man's thigh. She tried to keep it still on her own, but fractured pieces of bone rubbed against each other with every step. God, give me strength.

Julia raised her arm, and counted one, two, three steps to find the rhythm in the steps of the man who carried her. On the fourth step, she stabbed with all her might. The blade dug deep into the soft tissue on the back of his left knee.

Screaming, the man fell to his knees. The uneven undergrowth and the weight of the girl on his shoulder made him fall forward. Julia held on to the dagger as they fell. She slipped off his back and landed on her knees in front of him. As the man lifted his upper body to get to his feet, she thrust the blade under his jaw.

'For Mother,' she said.

The man tried to speak, his eyes wide with shock and terror. Julia pulled out the knife and watched the blood run down his throat. She felt so strong, as if nourished by his blood and life force.

'For Father!'

She stabbed again, just below the first wound. Her foe screamed again, without words. A strange, rattling sound. The blood flowed from his mouth.

'For Marcus!'

She twisted the dagger, and pulled it out with a gush of blood. The man no longer screamed.

'For me!'

Chapter 16: Hoy

Eight ships left Sanday in the rain the next morning, including the three ships from Horthaland, who attacked Wucestre. Sigurd Jarl's vessel led the way, followed by Magnus Trygg's ship, with Ulv and Marcus aboard. The crew had changed from the trip north. Geir Galne, Vass and half a dozen other berserks were also on board.

Kjetil Korte commanded the third ship behind them. Ulv had watched him say goodbye to his family. The whole scene was unexpected, Ulv had not even imagined that Kjetil had a family. However, standing on the beach was a nice-looking woman, and five kids, including two daughters who seemed to be a bit younger than Ulv. The youngest kids cried and hugged their father.

All the same, Ulv was pleased to avoid the unpleasant half-giant, and hoped for a more comfortable voyage this time, despite the wind and rain. It was always windy on the Nordreyjar, and it would be even worse when they came on the open sea.

The ships lay in a line, snaking between the small islands. Ulv stole a look at a crude map before they left, and tried to follow the mental representation of the route along the way. They sailed south around Eday, west through the strait between Egilsay and Westray, until the sea lay open in front of them. Several ships came from other islands and joined the line before they all turned south along the coast to Stromness.

There, they were met by more ships, and they were among the last of about forty vessels when they crossed the strait of Hoy and sailed towards the land of the Picts, with the high cliffs on the port side.

'Are you ready to prove your manhood?' Geir Galne asked.

Ulv shifted his gaze from the waves hitting the cliffs, and discovered to his surprise that Galne looked straight at him. The berserk shifted his gaze and pointed at a tall, slender rock rising, solitary from the sea. The height had to be about eight ship-lengths. Like a man standing with his arms crossed over his chest and scouting across the ocean.

' "The old man". All grown men among us have climbed it.'

Ulv gazed from the stone man to the warriors around him. Some nodded eagerly, others grunted affirmations.

'Pretty easy in the summer, really. "The man" was covered in ice when I climbed,' one said.

'I had only seen eight winters when I was up there for the first time,' another said.

'I forgot my shield on top, so I had to climb back up to fetch it. Then I had to dive from the peak to catch the ship before it sailed,' a third said.

Of course, it was probably all nonsense, but that was of little significance. Ulv had been dared. Challenged to prove himself a man. Or die trying. He glanced at the huge rock. Decades of rough weather, with lashing water and wind, had polished the stone. There was rain in the air, and the wind would tear and pull at any man trying to climb it. Ulv felt no enthusiasm for the task.

'Perhaps you're not a man?' Geir Galne asked, as no response came. 'You have a woman's courage. You fight like a woman, and I expect you to climb like a woman too.' He spat and turned away, as in disgust. His men chortled.

Ulv searched for a way out. Magnus Trygg sat in the stern and did not seem to care about the commotion. He saw no way out without attracting more dishonour and ridicule.

Getting to his feet, Ulv started to undress. If he was to have any energy left for the climb, he could not wear much for the swim. Removing shoes and garments, he soon stood in his underwear and belt. The sax hung in its scabbard, and he moved it further behind on the right side of the hip. After stowing the clothes in his ship's chest, he went to the rail and looked downhearted at the waves and the cold sea.

'I haven't climbed that either.'

Ulv turned and saw the young berserk called Vass getting up and undress. However, he did not stop until he was completely naked. His musculus frame revealed that he had climbed and swum many times before.

'That's because you're a Dane, boy. Get dressed and sit back down!'
Geir Galne did not seem content with the interference.

Vass did not even spare the old berserk a glance.

'Never will it be said that I lack a man's courage!' he said as he took
three steps and dived into the sea.

All was quiet for a moment until Vass appeared several man-lengths
further away. He lay flat with his head underwater and swam with gentle
strokes, one arm at a time. Sometimes turning his face up to the side and
breathing. He was halfway to the rock when Ulv took hold of the rail and
jumped.

Underwater he could not hear the laughter from the crew.

Not his first time swimming in the sea, he kept in control when the cold
shock came. Opening his eyes, he found himself surrounded by an unclear
blend of black, green and blue. It was bright above him. His wet pants
pulled his legs down towards the darkness below. It would be a tough swim,
but grown men were expected to be able to swim in the same clothes they
would wear in battle.

Kicking hard, he reached the surface and drew a deep breath. His eyes
found the stone man, and he adjusted the direction before he kicked off
again. The waves helped him forward until he reached the rocky shore at
the foot of the high cliff. Breathing heavy, he coughed before taking the
first careful steps towards the rock wall. The wind blew cold at his back,
and his wet hair was plastered to his face.

'Your swimming is not bad, but your shape is,' Vass said, leaning
against the rock wall.

Ulv tried to overlook the fact that the strong berserk was utterly naked.

'Thanks, I guess.'

Wasting no time Ulv searched with his fingers for handholds in the rock face and started the climb. He really wanted to avoid having Vass above him as he ascended.

Finding holds for fingers and toes was easy. The rock wall consisted of layers of stone slates that were stacked on top of each other. Each stone the width of one to ten hands. However, Ulv soon realised that the sandstones were wet and slippery, and sometimes pieces broke off at the edges. His fingers crawled over the cracks above him, and he felt slick mud several places. He began moving sideways around the cliff, towards the east side not as exposed to wind and sea.

The wall became steeper and leaned outwards in several places. But the rocks seemed firmer, and a narrow fissure went all the way to the top. In the cleft, sheltered from the wind, they climbed with one foot on either side of the crack.

For a while, it went well, but he had never climbed such a distance before. Soon his muscles ached, and his arms got heavier for every step. He tried to rest when he had firm holds for his toes, but Vass did not share a similar view about stopping. He patted Ulv on his leg or commanded 'Move on!' as soon as he reached him. 'You can rest at the top or in the boat, not here!'

Being heavier than Ulv, Vass breathed hard when they started on the last section. On this part the cliff wall leaned outwards, the stone was smoother and had fewer and shallower cracks. They kept following the cleft and Ulv focused on the next handhold. Then the next. And the next.

At last, Ulv put his arm over to the top, and felt the grass between his fingers. After pulling himself up, he lay flat on the grass, breathing. The plateau was a small area, no more than fifteen to twenty steps across. It slanted a bit with the highest point facing the ocean to the west. Vass seemed to have gained new energy from reaching the top because he quickly got on his feet and walked to the edge. He pointed skywards with both arms and shouted something Ulv did not understand. Ulv had not thought about the ship and crew as they climbed, but he did not hear any response from down there.

Worried he got up, walked over to Vass and looked down at the ships. He was not prepared for the sight that met him. The sea terrible far below. The sinking feeling in his gut so intense it seemed like his intestines were pulled into the ocean. Bending forward, he felt dizzy and nauseated from the height and exertion.

Vass took him by the arm and pulled him back.

'I don't think it's a good idea to dive from here,' he said with a slight smile.

'I'll try not to,' Ulv murmured and lay down on his stomach. Then, he pulled himself to the edge and realised that they had more significant problems than the height. To the south-west, he saw the colourful sails of three dozen ships. Further south, the north coast of the land of the Picts. Below them and to the right, to the north along the rocky shores of the coast they sailed, he saw four ships, scattered with some distance between. The fleet sailed on, no one waited for them. The last vessels would pass before they would get down.

'We have a problem,' Ulv said.

'I would say you're right. Perhaps we should dive from here after all?' Once again, the berserk smiled.

'What if we can't get to the ships?'

'Swim after them, or swim back to Sanday,' Vass answered.

This time he did not smile, and Ulv was not sure whether he actually meant it or not. Shaking his head, he went back to the spot where they climbed on to the plateau. The chance of getting aboard one of the ships would be less and less the longer they waited. Without looking down, he lay down on to his stomach, put his feet over the edge and searched for footholds.

'We should've had a rope,' he said but regretted it as he lifted his gaze towards Vass. There the berserk stood, still completely naked, with a thoughtful expression on his face and patting his body where pockets usually would be found. For the first time, Ulv noticed that the young warrior's chest, stomach and legs were covered by small cuts and bruises after the climb.

Vass searched under one arm, then the other, before his face lit up with eagerness as he examined his groin.

'Good luck with that,' Ulv said dryly before he lowered his body down over the edge. He held his upper body close to the wall while he searched around for cracks for his toes. His feet were bloody and numb, and it was hard to decide if edges and crevices could be used as holds.

In the next moment, Ulv lost his grip with both hands. For what seemed like an eternity, he scratched for handholds, while his toes started to slip. Then, his toes could not bear his weight anymore, and he began to slide down the rock face. He knew the speed would pick up. Knew he had no chance of getting hold of anything. Knew he was doomed.

A firm hand clasped his left wrist. And before he knew it, he was lifted, almost straight up, to the plateau again.

Without further ceremony, Vass threw his legs over the edge. 'I'm going first.' He glanced up at Ulv. 'You will not be able to hold on if I fall down on top of you.'

'But you do?' Ulv asked in a low voice. However, no answer was forthcoming. Vass had started the descent. Ulv took a few deep breaths, trying to control his hammering heart and knotted stomach. He threw a last glance at the two sails he could see from the east side of the cliff and started climbing down for the second time.

It took just as long to climb down as up. Two of the ships Ulv had seen from the top passed before they reached halfway down. With the wind lashing against them, they did not even try to shout. Ulv was tired. So very tired. He turned and gazed north following every step he took – no more sails. Fingers and toes were aching and bloody, and desperation gnawed at him like a stream eroding a sandbank. Putting his foot down on something soft, he looked down and met Vass's gaze.

'Sorry!' Ulv said, moving his foot from the berserks hand. Closing his eyes, he rested against the rock wall for a heartbeat or two. When he opened his eyes and turned, he saw something red and white coming into view by the coast in the north. One last ship! Hope and energy came rushing back, and he moved his hands and feet in a hurry to get down.

'Ai!' exclaimed Ulv, when first one foot, then the other foot, slipped. He hung from the fingers on his left hand and flailed with his legs in a feeble attempt to find a foothold. His bloody fingers started sliding off the stone. He realised that this was not going to end well. A cry erupted from his open mouth.

At the last instance, his right foot found a hold so he could put weight on it while tightening the grip with his fingers. Looking down, he saw Vass standing below him, with his right foot on a shelf and his right arm in a cleft. With his left hand, he held around Ulv's ankle, keeping the foot steady on a small ledge.

'Yes, I do,' he said, in response to the question Ulv asked at the top, 'but if we are to dive, we should move around on the other side. From there we have a hope of landing in the sea.'

He relaxed the hold on Ulv and started climbing to the right. Ulv followed, trembling and unsteady, but soon they had water below. It was at least eight man-lengths down.

Without saying a word, Vass let go of the rock and threw himself head first against the waves. In a heartbeat, Ulv had plenty of time to worry about whether the berserk would hit rock or water.

Vass stretched out his arms just before he hit the water and disappeared. Ulv was relieved but not surprised when the young man appeared in the waves swimming hard to intercept the ship with the red and white sail. Ulv planted his feet the best he could and jumped. A rush of air and the shock of impact. His legs were forced up against his body, and the breath struck from his lungs.

He sank deep.

Ulv flailed with arms and legs until his foot hit something. The bottom. Planting his feet on the rocky surface, he kicked off. His heart thundered, and his chest expanded to pull down air he could not reach. He stretched his arm against the light and pumped his legs with fervour. Suddenly he broke the surface. Ulv gasped for air as if trying to fill his lungs with all the air in the world at the same time. A wave struck him, and he drew in seawater.

Water all around him again. His breathing was out of control, and he pulled in more water.

His arms and legs would not cooperate. The sea closed above him.

Chapter 17: Viking

Marcus quickly understood that the challenge did not concern him. He was a slave, and would not be recognised as a man in the eyes of the heathens, no matter where he climbed or what he accomplished. It turned out to be a correct assessment. No one looked at him. He sat down on a seaman's chest and watched as Ulv reached land a while after the berserk. Ulv began to climb first, but for some reason, he stopped and began to move to the left, away from the sea. The crew laughed out loud as if they assumed the boy had already given up.

When the ship passed the lonely cliff, Magnus Trygg changed course. Instead of following the south lane the other vessels followed, they lay to the west. The crew took to the oars, rowing in a wide arc. They returned towards the coast some distance north of the cliff. By then, almost all the other ships had passed, and only a few vessels lay behind them in the north. The crew was all quiet when they passed 'The Old Man' for the second time. Everyone watched the cliff, looking for the two who took the challenge from Geir Galne. No one laughed.

Trygg did not change course this time but followed the other ships towards the coast of the land of the Picts.

Marcus thought about what it would mean for him if Ulv did not return. He was Ulv's slave. Without Ulv, he would still be a slave. But whose? They could sell him and share the spoils. But as far as he understood, they were now on a raid, and would not stop to sell anyone until they had fought a great battle. Of course, they could sell him along with the other slaves after the battle. If they managed to keep him alive for that long. He looked towards land and tried to calculate the distance. The ships further ahead stayed close to shore. Would he be able to swim ashore from the ship, if he waited until they got closer to land?

'Have you ever seen a Pict, boy?'

Marcus startled and turned towards the voice. Magnus Trygg stood behind him and gazed towards land with a thoughtful expression. Marcus repeated the sounds of the words to himself until he recognised most.

'No, my father said Picti live north of our country. Before, war. Now, peace.' He struggled to find the right words.

'They paint. Picti.' The last word he uttered with greater force and confidence. It was a word from Latin, the language of his forefathers. A strange pride rose in him as he spoke it.

Trygg looked down at him and nodded appreciatively. 'How did you learn our language?'

'My father was a merchant. He traded with many people, Northmen as well, until three years ago. He spoke many languages. Father taught my sister and me. Many words, but not everything. We understand a lot, but we speak poorly.'

Trygg seemed curious now. 'How did he teach you the language?'

Marcus took his time, pausing to think of each sentence before pronouncing it. 'From when we were little. We learned several names for the same thing. We learned three words that were *knife*. Three words that were *cow*. Three words that were *ships*. But we did not know which languages. We spoke Norse one day or Latin five days. Father taught us common words. Two hundred. Maybe three hundred.'

'Your father was a wise man. So you know several languages?'

'Yes. Latin. My father's language. Words there too. Father taught us to read some texts. We can write a little. But no one else speaks Latin now. Except in the Church. The language of the priests is similar, but not the same as ours.'

'Was your father a man of the Church before he became a merchant?' If Trygg wondered who Marcus meant by saying *we*, he did not reveal it by any means.

'No, my father was always a merchant, but my father …' Marcus tried to find a word he knew he did not know. 'My many father's father was a great Roman man in Britain. Our family honours him.'

'A family that values learning and honour,' said Trygg nodding.

Marcus felt proud for a brief moment before he again realised that he himself was the last man of his house. And now a slave. He glanced towards land and changed the subject.

'Have you seen the Picti?'

Trygg made a short sound as if laughing. There was no sign of joy in his face. His gaze fixed on the shore.

'Yes, I have seen many Picts. Awful many.'

Feeling that the Northman was not finished, Marcus did not say anything.

After a long silence, Magnus Trygg continued. 'Awful many. We fought a large battle against them two winters ago. They gathered the clans in the north. Many fell, and they lost many of their kings and great men. We won, but many brave men were taken to Valhall that day.'

Trygg stood still for a while, before turning around and walking aft in the ship again. Marcus had lost interest in swimming. He looked down at the planks beneath him and the hopelessness took hold of him once more.

*

'Do you know what we do with small, useless puppies?'

Marcus looked up and gazed straight into Geir Galne's wide-open eyes.

'We drown them!' Galne hissed.

To reinforce the message, he pretended to grab something with both hands and throw it over the railing.

'Plop. Blubblubblubb.'

The last sounds he made with his lips a finger's breadth from Marcus's nose. Galne continued to stare with bloodshot, bulging eyes from close range. Marcus did not dare wipe the saliva from his face.

'Thank you,' Marcus said quietly, getting up and moving away.

He needed the reminder. Julia was a prisoner at Torgils, on one of the ships further ahead. Even if he managed to escape from the boat, and swim to the land of the Picts, he would have little chance of survival. And no chance of helping Julia. Right now, he was a slave on his way to the Green Isle. But he assumed that it would not be long before the crew got bored, discerning that the masterless slave would do more good as a sacrifice to the sea god they called Njord. Marcus realised that he had to take his share of the chores on board if he was to survive the voyage. He had spent many days on the ship and observed what tasks the crew had.

Marcus was on the same ship in which he had left the village. He had seen both larger and smaller vessels on Sanday, but most were larger. The mast stood in the middle of the ship, and the sail was as usual hoisted. The ship was the same forward and aft, so it could be sailed or rowed both ways. This ship had six pairs of oars, with three rows of sea chests in front and three rows behind the mast. Only on three occasions had the crew rowed, and then only for a short while.

Barrels of water, beer and wine were tied down in the bow. Wheat, barley, apples and dried meat stored aft. During the trip to the Orkneyjar, they ate porridge or gruel of barley, with some dried meat. They restocked on the islands, and both food and drink were much better now. Ulv and Marcus had been sitting on Ulv's ship's chest in the middle of the vessel. Marcus, of course, had no ship's chest, but then he owned nothing either. Ulv had his place by the oars just behind the mast, on the starboard side.

At night, the crew slept in pairs on deck, in leather sleeping bags that were fastened together to better keep the warmth. Marcus had not received a sleeping bag on his way to the Orkneyjar, but on this raid, he hoped that he could use Ulv's when night came.

With Geir Galne and his berserks, there had been twenty men on board. Now they were two less. The berserks were perhaps more undisciplined, but otherwise, Marcus did not notice any difference between them and the rest of the crew. After Magnus Trygg killed the two berserks on their voyage from Wucestre, no one had shown him any disrespect.

Marcus gathered his courage and stepped over the ship's chests on the way aft. Kneeling down in front of Trygg, he lowered his eyes and waited for permission to speak. He did not know if this was how these heathens showed humility, but as a Christian, it felt natural. The fact that he just had a normal conversation with the same man bore no significance.

'Talk!' Trygg did not waste time on formalities.

'My master is not here. I ask, can I do his work?'

Marcus grimaced. He regretted the choice of words. He should have spent more time finding the right phrases to express such an important message. He did not dare look up. It was all quiet behind him, and he realised he had put Trygg in a difficult spot. Trygg had been accused of being too soft, and last time he had to kill two men. Why should he risk his own life or the lives of others, by having an incompetent Northumbrian doing important tasks on their way to a great battle? Marcus pondered once more how he would fare swimming towards the land of the Picts. *Blubblubblubb*, as Geir Galne said.

'You will do his work on board,' Trygg replied. He raised his voice to drown out the murmur from the crew. 'You must do his job,' he repeated, 'you must dress in his armour and carry his weapon. You shall fight the battle in his stead, and you shall honour your master. By your skill and honour, both of you will be judged by gods and men.'

There were some dissatisfied grunts, then some mumblings. Marcus sat still until Trygg nudged him with his foot. He got up, bowed, and climbed back over the ship's chests.

He would live a few more days. But then he would go into battle. As a Viking. With enemies on all sides.

Chapter 18: Fools

A dark, blurry line rippled and curled in contrast to the light above.

Ulv stretched towards it, felt something tangible against his fingers and grabbed hold. Nothing happened. He pulled his hands towards his face and saw that the shadow was a rope. It must have fallen out of one of the ships that passed.

The rope almost slipped through his fingers as it tightened. With both hands on the line, Ulv held on for his life and was dragged through the water. Swirling and spinning, and with his eyes closed, he did not know if he was pulled up or down. He did not care. His whole body screamed for one last inhale, but he resisted the overwhelming urge, which would only fill his lungs with seawater.

Air graced his face for a moment before a wave struck him. More air, another wave. Something squeezed his wrists, and he was pulled up from the water. Ulv coughed and gasped for air.

Seawater poured out of his nose and mouth. Exhausted, he fell on his back. Through blurry eyes, he saw dancing colours. Red and white.

Sails.

Someone spoke, and Ulv turned towards the sound. He blinked and shook his head.

An old warrior stood over him, his arm outstretched. The man even older than Magnus Trygg. Dazed, Ulv accepted the outstretched hand. The grip was surprisingly firm, and he was almost lifted on to his feet. The man introduced himself as Ragnar.

'Did you reach the top?' he asked in a sharp and clear voice, nodding towards the rocks behind them.

'Yes,' Ulv answered while studying the man. Grey hair and beard surrounded a tanned and weather-beaten face.

'Impressive,' Ragnar answered and nodded. 'And foolish,' he continued without a hint of a smile. He shifted his gaze from Ulv to Vass. 'Young warriors must learn not to be foolish if they want to become old warriors. Besides, I have no room for fools on this ship.' He moved his eyes back to Ulv. 'Was it a dare, a challenge or test of manhood?' But instead of waiting for a reply, he answered the question himself. 'A test of manhood I'll guess. So, either you have a poor position among the crew, or you're just crazy. Since I had to pick you up, I'm guessing the first.' He looked at Ulv.

'Close enough,' mumbled Ulv, too tired for guessing games.

'I am, however, just a fool,' Vass answered with his usual grin.

'Oh well. I can live with a competent fool and a capable youngster. Get out of those wet rags and find yourself a blanket.'

*

They huddled under blankets when Vass spoke.

'How did you manage to win the duel against Kjetil?'

'I don't really know,' Ulv said, thinking. 'He was too confident, too impatient, too predictable.'

'But he is a great warrior. One of Sigurd's most respected men.'

'Yes. But he is easy to read. He lowers his left shoulder before slashing his sword diagonally from right to left, he lifts his shield before stabbing and comes out to the left with the shield before hacking straight down.'

Vass nodded slowly. 'For how long have you studied him? I thought this was your first raid?'

'Yes, it is my first raid. But I didn't need to watch him for long. It was quite obvious. Father taught me to fight differently. I wasn't big, or strong enough, so he taught me to take advantage of my speed. We practised, and I trained to get even faster. The training made me think quicker too. We didn't waste time trying to work on something I couldn't master anyway,' he said.

Vass nodded again. 'But there weren't many who liked the way you fought,' he said with a smile.

'I noticed,' Ulv replied dryly. 'Father warned me about that, that I didn't fit in. That I should stay away. Stay away as he had done.'

'As he had done?' Vass answered with another question.

'Father is, well, he is not …' Ulv realised how much he was about to tell Vass. But what did he have to lose? Vass was one of the few friendly souls he had met. It was good to talk without thinking about the consequences. He had tried to find the right words to achieve the right things all too often lately. And he had nothing to show for it. Still, he kept some things for himself. He did not have to share everything at once.

'Father taught me a lot. To fight, but not like a warrior. To hunt, to shoot with the bow. But over the last few years, I became impatient. I wanted to meet more people. I couldn't keep living in the woods. When father was gone, what would I do? No, I had to do something before it was too late.'

They sat in silence for a while. 'Father didn't teach me much about the outside world. He said I didn't fit in, but I thought it was just something he said so I wouldn't leave him. I had an idea. I would make sure that an important man understood that he needed me. Sigurd Jarl fitted the image I had in mind. I would convince him to take me in as one of his men. Sigurd Jarl was in a feud with Hundolf the Jarl of Gaular. So I decided to give Sigurd a gift. Something belonging to Hundolf.'

'I went to Hundolf's farm and began detailing a plan. I hid in the tall grass on a small hill a bowshot away. From there, I had a good view of the farm. Hundolf had a great longhouse where the men gathered in the evenings. Later, most left with unsteady steps. House thralls came and went with buckets and troughs. In the evening, I drew back from the farm and slept under an evergreen. When darkness fell the second day, I had a simple plan.'

'I gathered twigs and moss and climbed to the roof. I scrambled up at the corner furthest from the door, which was partially covered by a large birch. From there, I followed the ridge of the roof and used what I had gathered to plug the chimney. The idea was that it would cause more smoke to be trapped inside the house. I hid behind the nearby bathhouse. And waited.'

Ulv was quiet for a moment. Then he raised his voice and continued at a faster pace.

'The door went up. A thrall came out with a bucket. Limping slightly on his left foot. Impatient, I took my chance. I picked up a bucket lying around at the chicken coop. The hens clucked a warning, but no one reacted. On my way to the door, I started to limp. Hoping that nobody would spare a second glance for a thrall coming in.'

'I slipped through the door but needed time to get my bearings. I put the bucket down and turned my back to the room to close the door. It smelled of smoke, charred meat and sweat. I lowered my head, but instead of fixing my eyes to the ground, I gazed ahead beneath my eyebrows.'

Ulv imitated his own description. Vass smiled. Ulv continued, calmly.

'Satisfied, I noticed that there was a lot of smoke and little light in the room. I stayed to the side of the room while ambling towards the fireplace. The Jarl was easily recognisable, and I was looking for something that stood out, on him or close to him. My proof. He sat, talking loudly with three other men. As I approached the end of the table, I saw his sword hanging from the belt. It appeared to be a fine sword, but most likely not distinct enough to be identified as his. Besides, it was not easy to steal a sword.'

Ulv pretended to hold something long and be searching for a place on his body where he could place it. An expression of deep concentration on his face.

Several of the other crew members stopped what they were doing. The boat was quiet when Ulv continued his tale, his neck bent and eyes looking around.

'With my head low and a frantic gaze, I kept searching. I would soon pass him by. Before much time passed, I had to be out of there if I were to get away. Then I discovered the goblet the Jarl drank from. It was silver, with a warrior carrying a shield and a spear. It would stand out! However, it would not be easier to steal a mug from a hand than a sword from a belt. I was out of time like a boy who has thrown stones on a wasp nest, so I grabbed the first opportunity I got.'

'A female thrall came towards the table with a jug of beer. I turned my face away from her, as I set the course closer to the table and towards her.'

Ulv turned his head to the right and leaned to the left. Once again, he increased the pace of the story.

'Two more steps and we would pass each other. I took a deep breath and risked everything. I stumbled against her and pushed both her and the jug of beer towards the table where the Jarl and the other men sat.'

'The thrall girl cried out, and I followed her motion towards the table as if I tried to hold her up. Just before we fell over, I steadied myself on the edge of the table. While the men were busy with the woman who came tumbling down and the beer that was floating over the table like a tide ...'

'Swoosh ...' Ulv continued as he stroked the imaginary table to imitate the beer as a flood.

'I grabbed the Jarl's goblet and slipped it into my bag. I whispered a hasty excuse and hurried further into the house while mumbling something about finding a rag to clean up. After a few steps, I stopped and looked around ...'

Ulv looked around, confused.

'I took a bucket and walked towards the door. The woman kept rambling apologies. Halfway to the door, I realised I was supposed to have a limp. The men talked loudly in each other's mouths. I was fast approaching the door.'

'The door went up and the thrall I was supposed to be, came in ...'

Ulv paused his storytelling for a moment before he continued:

'I didn't take the chance to wait, so I pushed through the door at the same time he entered, and we passed as we stared at each other from inches apart. Afterwards, I felt his eyes on my neck, and I was expecting an outcry. When I rounded the corner of the house, I let go of the bucket and ran.'

'That was some story,' Vass said with a smile, when Ulv had been quiet for a moment. 'When you're done playing warrior, you can earn your living as a skald!'

Ulv smiled. He was not sure why he changed the end of the story at the last minute. He just knew he was not ready to tell that part. Not yet.

'So, my great skald, cunning thief, fumbling warrior,' Vass said with mock gravity, 'how did you end up raiding with Sigurd Jarl and all of us?'

Ulv thought, and continued reluctantly. He made this part of the story much shorter. The desire to embellish and tell a good story as father had done so many times was gone.

'Well, I brought the mug and met up with Sigurd Jarl. He was not impressed. That is, he was not impressed that I just stole the mug. It seemed like everything would be fine if I had just killed someone at the same time.'

Vass nodded as if he understood the point.

Ulv continued. 'I was told that I had no honour. Kjetil wanted to hand me over to Hundolf, or most of all, to kill me right away. In the end, I was given a second chance. To prove myself worthy. By joining Sigurd Jarl's raid and prove myself as a warrior. Something I'm not. The result was given.'

Ulv produced a genuine smile for the first time in what felt like ages.

Vass laughed. 'There is still hope!'

'What about you? I heard Geir Galne say you're a Dane? You don't sound like a Dane?'

'No, I've grown up in Vestfold, mostly. I was sent north when I was just a little boy. The grandfather of the house trained me. I do not know much, like you do. I can only fight.'

'Which you do with great skill. I saw you in the attack on the village.'

'Well, while fighting merchants, bakers and peasants, I'm decent, yes. Something else would be weird. They do a bunch of things I can't. I would've starved to death if I had to make a loaf of bread to survive!'

'Bake, you mean!'

'There you have it!'

'How did you end up as one of the Jarl's men?'

'Sigurd hired us. He wanted to have a group of professional warriors with him, I guess. So he hired Geir Galne and his men. Just after I'd joined them, really.'

'Yes, Geir Galne. How *gal* is Geir Galne?' Ulv asked, using the Norse word for crazy. 'Every time I talk to him, he tries to explain by speaking about dogs in various shapes and forms.'

'Ha ha, Geir is a little crazy. But dogs are quite understandable. The first time I spoke to him, he chatted away about a songbird. I still don't know what he meant. He sometimes makes decisions for reasons no one else understands. So, I guess he is not the easiest to figure out. But he is not worse than most warriors, I would say. And he has treated me well.'

Ulv nodded but was not particularly convinced. To him, Galne appeared as someone who could smile at you and slap your shoulder with one hand while he drove a knife under your ribs with the other.

Chapter 19: Magnus Maximus

'This is our target!' Magnus Trygg said, pointing with his knife at a red line on the tanned goat hide fastened to the mast. Most of the crew sat close together on the ship's chests or watched from the stern. The leather had a rough outline of the Green Isle drawn on it, with some red rings and lines.

'Sigurd Jarl's three ships will row up the river Boyne, and further up the Blackwater, to Kells. The monks of Kvitekrist have a monastery there. Our job is to plunder this monastery and bring supplies back to the coast.'

'Supplies?' asked Arngrim, one of the few crewmembers Marcus knew by name. He uttered the word with an expression as if he had eaten something foul.

'Yes, supplies,' Trygg replied. 'If you find gold or gemstones, all the better. But Torgils has pillaged the area many times, and we must expect the Irish to have moved or hidden their remaining valuables. There might not be much left for us, and we have neither the time nor space for thralls. Our task is to obtain supplies for the raiding fleet. The monasteries collect and store food from the surrounding area. That is what we need to get.'

A dozen very dissatisfied Vikings shouted as one:

'Why?'

A couple of the crew spat and turned their backs to their chieftain. Marcus noticed that Trygg remained remarkably calm. He was a wise leader of men, who did not undermine his authority fighting petty squabbles.

'Because we are going to spend the winter on the Green Isle, and we need the food to survive,' Trygg replied, pronouncing each word a little slower and clearer than usual.

Again, he had everyone's attention. The Vikings always arrived early in the summer, sometimes also towards the end of the summer. But come winter they were gone. Marcus had no idea what the heathens were doing in the winter. He assumed they were fighting someone – quite possibly each other.

'We are sailing with a great fleet. Some ships will sail up the rivers, like us, attacking farms or monasteries. Øystein Glumra, the Jarl of Møre, will establish a winter camp here.'

With the knife, Trygg pointed at a red dot on the map, just above the red line representing the river Boyne.

'The Irish call the place Linn Duachaill. The small village will not offer resistance to Glumra. But soon, the Irish will unite against us. We are facing a long and hard winter.'

The crew fell silent, but their faces revealed that they were none too pleased with the plans. Magnus Trygg seized the opportunity to provide more details about the campaign.

'To the south' – he moved the knife to a ring at the end of a red line a hand's breadth further down the skin – 'Torgils and the Danes will attack Dyflin. The fighting will be hard. Torgils has been there several times before, and has even improved the fortifications himself. But he has never spent the winter there, thus allowing the Irish to return in his absence. They will expect another raid this year, but they don't know when. Torgils hopes that attacking more targets at the same time will prevent the Irish from gathering their forces.'

Trygg let the information sink in, and met the gaze of each crewmember in turn.

'Many will see the red sun for the last time tonight.'

Marcus had an overwhelming feeling he was among them. He turned to the sun, about to disappear into the sea for the last time. It was a warm late summer night. In other circumstances, it would have been a beautiful sunset. Not far away, men, women and children, would be watching the same sun, before going to sleep. Tomorrow, they would wake up to war cries and fires.

Twice, Marcus had experienced the horrors of a Viking raid. This time, he would fight side by side with the heathens from the north. He did not fear the Irish. The greatest threat to his own life was to be found among the men who were now inspecting their armour and weapons, getting ready for battle at first light.

Marcus decided to follow their lead and turned to Ulv's chest. It was not locked. He opened the lid tentatively, expecting somebody to be angered by a thrall taking such liberties. Nothing happened.

Inside were Ulv's tunic and pants, which he threw in the chest before he dove into the sea at Hoy. Marcus put on the pants but kept his own tunic.

Underneath, he found the padded coat of arms that Ulv had worn the morning they met in the cellar. It still stank of sour smoke. Marcus inspected it more closely and found that it was made from at least ten layers of wool and linen, sewn tightly together. Most of the warriors wore even thicker armour, providing better protection from arrows and swords. He pulled it over his head and tightened the straps.

Between the lower layers of clothing lay a beautiful silver drinking mug. Marcus studied it without taking it out of the chest. It was well made, with delicate decorations, and certain to be of great value. He let it lie. It would be safer in the chest. At the bottom, he also found a leather purse, with the arrowheads Ulv stole from the smiths at Sanday.

There was no weapon in the chest. Marcus had never practised archery, so the bow fastened on the outside of the chest would not be of use to him. Ulv had tied the long knife around his waist before he dived into the sea outside Hoy. Marcus had no idea whether the young Northman had fallen to his death, if he had been left behind or picked up by another ship. Marcus hoped for the latter, and that his new friend would use his seax well the following day.

In the bottom corner of the seaman's chest, he found an empty leather pouch, similar to the one containing the arrowheads. It might come in handy if he found something small of value. A ring from a monastery, or even a small gem, would keep him alive for a long time if he managed to get away from his current travel companions. Marcus quickly hung it around his neck and closed the lid, worried that he had not found a weapon he could use. The last rays of sun found his face as he crawled into Ulv's sleeping bag.

With the silence and the darkness came the fear and thoughts of what would happen the next day. Marcus was too anxious to sleep, but lay with his eyes closed, thinking of the life he had lived and what little remained of it. In the dark, he hoped no one would see his tears.

For comfort, Marcus clutched the leather pouch and realised that it was not completely empty. He untied the knot, loosened the thread, and emptied its contents in his hand.

Even in the sparse light, he recognised his father's ring, handed down from father to son for generations. It belonged to him now. Gently, he brushed over the seal with his fingers. "VIRTVS ROMANORVM" it said. And "MAG MAXIMVS". Magnus Maximus, his ancestor. The Roman general, who fought the Picts half a thousand years ago. Marcus found the comfort he was looking for. He put the ring on his finger and soon fell asleep.

Chapter 20: Dyflin

Ulv woke with a start. He had been dreaming. In his dream, he stood over Marcus, a blood-dripping knife in his hand. Marcus lay on his back, a large gaping wound in his stomach, the ground covered with blood. His eyes staring with a mixture of surprise and sorrow. It was not the first time Ulv dreamt this. What did it mean? Probably just that he felt terrible for killing Marcus's father. At the same time, he could not help thinking about the neighbour woman from back home. She was passionately concerned by dreams and what they meant. According to her, killing was the ultimate betrayal. Dreaming you killed someone meant you were going to let him or her down. Or was it the other way around, the murdered one who would betray the killer? Ulv did not remember. He had not paid much attention to what he considered being just foolish babbling from the old crone. He missed her. Missed the time when he and father stopped by her and traded meat, and sometimes hides for some extra eggs and butter. Life had been so much easier back then. Before he left his home because he was bored. By Odin's ravens, how he longed back to a dull, safe life.

It was still dark. His stomach ached. Not the kind of pain you would get from eating bad fish. No, this was worse. It was quiet on the boat that was anchored in a small bay not far from the village, which would soon experience the wrath of the Vikings. The great convoy had split, and Ulv and Vass would take part in the attack on the village nestled between two rivers on the shore of the Green Isles. The plan was to establish a camp for the winter. That was why they came in force. They had to be able to defend against any retaliation.

Ulv was not looking forward to the attack. This time he could not hide. He was off to a new start on this ship with Danes. Mostly because he was with Vass. Vass radiated overconfidence and strength, characteristics that resonated well with most Northmen warriors.

Along with Vass, and away from Sigurd Jarl and Kjetil Korte, Ulv was one of the crew. Thus, it was expected that he would contribute to the attack. He could not make a fool of himself with this crew as well. He had to take part. Had to fight. Kill or be killed. His stomach ached. It was still dark.

The night before, Ragnar brought equipment for Ulv and Vass. Most of their gear was left on Trygg's boat. Vass left everything, while Ulv had kept the seax. Earlier they received some clothes so they would not freeze – trousers and shirts of wool, and a pair of heavy cloaks. In addition, Ragnar brought over a bow, a quiver of arrows, and a weapon shirt. Vass had thanked him and given everything to Ulv. Ulv shot him a questioning look.

'I do not need the bow, but you do,' he said. Presenting his usual grin, he continued: 'You need it to cover me when I bite off more than I can chew'.

'Then you'll take my seax and the weapon shirt,' Ulv answered and started to loosen the belt the weapon hung from.

'Nope, the shirt does not fit, and the seax is yours. Besides, I don't want to be indebted to an *ulv*,' he said, using the Norse word for wolf.

He held up a hand, displaying a smile as wide as it was white. Ulv shook his head, but in all honesty, he was relieved.

Perhaps he could follow Vass at a distance and use his bow when an opening presented itself. He could not help but like the young berserk. At the same time, he was not sure if it was wise staying together with the reckless warrior. Vass had the skills to charge straight into the thick of battle, but Ulv did not have the experience to keep up.

Ulv came out of his reveries as the men around him began to stir. Ragnar walked around to those still sleeping and nudged them awake with his foot. Ulv got up and put his weapon shirt on. It was a bit large, but it would do. He examined the bow. It was shorter than the ones he was used to. He attached the bowstring and realised with satisfaction how powerful it was. Trying to draw it, he soon discovered that he was unable to pull it all the way back.

There were seventeen arrows in the quiver. The shafts were shorter than regular – convenient in a hectic battle. The bow was of good quality: no decorations or adornments, but a solid weapon. Ulv suspected the bow to be better than one would expect at first glance. Its unusual appearance and size were perhaps the reason why the warriors on board had overlooked it. Several of the warriors had bows, as it was customary that every other man on a ship was equipped with one.

A nearby warrior, a black-haired man with crooked teeth, glanced at Ulv.

'It belonged to a little devil from the east,' the warrior said.

Ulv just nodded.

'He shot faster than anyone I've ever seen,' the man continued. 'If you gave him a moment, you ended up looking like a hedgehog!' the warrior said and shook his head.

'Yes, he placed the arrows on the right side of the bow, on the thumb,' another warrior said as if it explained everything.

The tall, slender man turned back to the sleeping bag he tried to pack away. Ulv studied the bow once more thinking about what the Dane said. It made sense. Ulv, and everyone else he had seen, placed the arrows on the left side when nocking. It was inconvenient when speed was an issue. He tried to put an arrow on his thumb, as the tall warrior said. It felt wrong but should be possible with some work.

Ragnar's voice drew Ulv out of his contemplations.

'Get some food and get ready. We attack as soon as daylight lets us row the ships all the way up the beach. We, and three other ships, will follow the small river that flows south and west past the pool called Dyflin and debark on the south side. We go for speed and surprise, and we fight in groups of three. If we have to retreat, we meet on the grassy plain just north of where the river bends off to the south again, a few bow shots from the ships.'

It was common practice to have a meeting point away from the ships where one could regroup and strike back. When the Vikings pulled back, it seemed chaotic and uncoordinated, with warriors running in all directions. The pursuers, on the other hand, were in for a surprise when they realised that a large group of Vikings had reorganised and were ready to fight once more.

'Torgils's orders are to kill everyone who resists. Those who are not a threat can be captured. But get rid of everyone who may be a problem immediately,' continued the Dane. The ships that were to take part in the attack had settled side by side so that the leaders could meet on Torgils's ship.

'Torgils and Aud want to convert those willing to concede that Odin the Allfather is greater than Kvitekrist.'

Several of the warriors exchanged looks, some with surprise plain in their expressions, others with displeasure. Ragnar continued.

'But that is their problem, and only when the battle is over will we bother with such. Until then, we do not take any chances.'

If the attack on the little village Marcus lived in was bloody, this would be a lot worse. And he had to take part in the bloodshed. Kill or be killed.

Not long after, the ship drew away from the convoy and followed the little river south. On top of a slope to the right, they saw lights from the village. The river swung westward, and they now had the town on the right side, and the pool stretched out to the left. Towards the town, the slope was still steep, but a bit further in it became gentler, and here they debarked. Ulv and Vass had not received any special instructions. Ulv glanced at Vass while they were waiting to jump ashore. Vass had taken off his wool shirt and stood there barefoot, without weapons and only wearing a pair of green woollen trousers. His body was scratched after the climb, and Ulv suddenly felt the sting from his own wounds from the perils on the rock.

'And you've taken off your wool shirt because …?'

Vass glanced back at Ulv. 'It's itchy when I get warm.'

Then he smiled back. 'Stay some way behind me when the battle begins, but keep in sight,' he continued, hopping ashore.

Ulv jumped after, and the group started climbing up the hill. Towards the top of the slope, Ragnar signalled the men to keep low. They dropped down on all four and crept to the top, where they hid behind some large stones. From the rocks, they saw the village, and the closest buildings were just a bowshot away. Ragnar gave the order to wait until they heard an alarm or that the fight started. To their right, back to the east and above the pool they sailed past, they could see that a part of the village lay behind a palisade. There, the slopes down to the water were steeper, making it the best protected part of the town.

Ulv glanced down at his hands. He held the bow in one hand and three arrows in the other. He tightened the grip on the weapons, trying to force his hands to stop shaking. He glanced at the warriors. Most bore swords or axes in hand, some had shields at the ready, while others still had them on their backs. Some looked angry. Not Kjetil Korte-angry, but more controlled. Others seemed afraid, more as he expected he looked himself. Wide eyes, open mouth and nostrils. Still, others looked focused. Vass, on the other hand, he closed his eyes, murmuring something. Then he opened them, took a few quick breaths, clapped himself on his cheeks and tightened the muscles in his upper body. Finally, the smile came back. Ulv felt an urge to do something similar. As if it would make him better prepared.

He settled for trying to look more angry than scared.

As the sunrise coloured the sky blood red, a roar sounded from the other side of the village. Warriors who roared in unison did little to calm the maelstrom in Ulv's stomach.

'It is time,' Ulv heard to his left. The sharp, yet calm, voice of Ragnar. The old man was quickest on his feet and set away towards the buildings. The clattering from chain mails, the trampling of feet and the breath of men were all that could be heard. Ulv dragged behind. Vass was in front. His feet and upper body bared, and without weapons.

A cry sounded from in between the houses. They had been discovered.

Vass veered right, away from the others. He set course towards two villagers who had arrived between a couple of circular houses. Ulv dropped down to one knee, stuck two arrows in the ground in front of him and nocked the third. He lifted his bow and gaze to Vass and the two men. One held a pitchfork. The other, who came a little further behind, had an axe. Vass did not slow down. The man with the pitchfork, a tall, stocky man, stood with his right foot in front of him and pulled the pitchfork back with both hands. As he stabbed, Vass took two steps to the left. The pitchfork poked two holes in the air where Vass had just been. Vass turned towards the man, grabbed the fork in his right hand and, as he twisted around, slammed his left elbow in the man's temple.

Ulv pulled back the string and aimed his first arrow at the man further back. The man moved calmly towards Vass. Ulv took a deep breath and let the arrow fly. The arrow whistled through the air.

And missed. With a thud, the arrow sank into a cart in front of the house behind the man. Ulv looked at his hands – they still shook.

Fortunately, Vass was in control. He twisted all the way around and stood facing the axeman with the pitchfork in front of him. The owner of the pitchfork lay still on the ground. Ulv drew an arrow from the ground and nocked it. The man with the axe lifted the weapon over his head and chopped down at Vass. Vass turned the fork upwards and parried with the opening that lacked its middle tip. Ulv aimed, but held the arrow. Vass twisted the fork around its own axis, pinning the axe between the two remaining peaks, and kept turning until the weapon spun out the man's hands. The axe fell to the ground, and Vass followed up by pulling the pointed end of the fork to him and downwards. The back end struck the man's chin. The man went to the ground.

Vass glanced down at the pitchfork and nodded with a satisfied expression on his face. He waved Ulv forward and continued in between the buildings with his new weapon. Ulv hurried after, leaving the men behind. Both were knocked out, but probably not dead. Ulv was both worried and happy about that fact and loped after Vass.

They ran between more of the circular buildings without encountering resistance – Vass in front, Ulv behind. Sounds of battle could be heard in front of them. Rounding a house, they met four Irishmen turning another building, only thirty steps away from him and fifteen from Vass. These were young, strong men, with swords and axes. One of the men smiled, apparently happy to run into a single Viking with a broken pitchfork as his only weapon. Ulv sat down carefully on one knee, hoping to remain undiscovered while the men focused on the half-naked young man. He stuck two arrows in the ground in front of him and nocked a third.

One of the men came running towards him. Ulv lifted the bow and aimed. One shot was all he would get. The arrow flew, and he knew his aim to be true this time. The man leapt to the side, and the shaft passed him by. He smiled, seemingly pleased with his lucky timing, and the advantage he now held. The axe came swinging, angling down towards Ulv. Ulv dropped the bow and rolled to the left. A heartbeat later he was back on his feet with the seax in hand. The man did not look so confident anymore, but he came forward with his back bent and the axe at the ready.

Ulv had to finish this quickly. However skilled Vass was with a pitchfork as a weapon, he was alone against three, and poorly equipped.

The man took a quick step forward and chopped with the axe from up high. Ulv jumped backwards in the last instance. He hesitated and kept going back to lure the axe-man forward. The feint worked almost too well. The next swing came from close in. Ulv could not jump away. Instead, he took a step forward so that the attack would lose momentum and power when the man's arm slowed against the left side of Ulv's body. Ulv stepped backwards with his right foot, giving himself room to stab with the knife towards the man's gut. Avoiding looking the man in the face, he pushed him away and to the ground. He lifted his gaze and found Vass. One of the men lay on his back and was out of the fight. The other two circled him in a way that meant that Vass was in trouble. Ulv found the bow, nocked the arrow and pulled back the string as he turned. One of the men had his back against Ulv. Vass was in the middle, and the other man seemed to prepare for an attack. Ulv knew that the other warrior would follow up with another attack just after.

Ulv aimed squarely at the man's back, breathed calmly, and let the arrow fly.

Chapter 21: Boyne

'Are you going to stare the monks to death, or strangle them with your bare fists?' Magnus Trygg did not wait for an answer.

'Give the boy a weapon,' he commanded. He turned to Marcus. 'Sword, axe or spear?'

'Axe!' Marcus replied, without revealing that by the Viking's standards, he was utterly helpless no matter what weapon he got his hands on. The next moment, an axe came flying towards him in the dim morning light. Marcus waved his arms in front of him, as he could not decide whether to catch the axe in the air or to defend himself from being hit. He hit the wooden shaft, making it spin over his right forearm, before it fell towards the ship's deck, with the curved blade first. By reflex, his left hand grabbed the shaft, stopping the weapon from hitting the floor.

The manoeuvre was met by chuckles and laughter.

'Deft!' whispered Arngrim. 'It's an axe, not a wasp, boy!'

More chuckles. Marcus weighed the axe in his hand and could not decide whether he would be able to swing it with one hand. It was not tempting to go into battle without a shield, or something else to hide behind. A new wave of fear came flushing in when he thought about what would happen this morning. He was about to fight Irishmen defending their homes. He might have to kill a Christian who protected his family, who did what he did not dare just nine days before. He might be killed, or badly injured. Lifting the axe, Marcus thought about how painful it would be to get hit by such a weapon in the knee. Or shoulder. Or the head. He shuddered at the thought.

'Man the oars!' Trygg commanded, keeping his voice low.

It was quiet in the boat, and no sounds were heard from the crews in the other vessels either. The Green Isle lay dark and shapeless in front of them. Some ships had broken out of the column and rowed ashore. Now there were half a dozen ships left, sailing straight towards a settlement nestled on either side of the mouth of a large river, the Boyne. Marcus loosened one of the shields hanging over the railing, and slung it over his back, as he had seen the other oarsmen do. It felt safer to be protected by a shield. He found his place on Ulv's ship's chest and threaded the oar through the hole under the railing.

Marcus lifted his gaze and saw a vessel behind them. The unrest rose in him. He knew Kjetil Korte was on board that ship. In front of them was Sigurd Jarl's boat. Soon the front three ships would go ashore, and the last three – the same ones who attacked Wucestre – would grow further up the river Boyne. Towards the monastery of Kells.

Magnus Trygg gave the order to tie up the sail.

'Row!' he commanded, at the same moment that a church bell began to toll at a rapid pace.

They had been discovered. Marcus took his first, faltering strokes on the heavy oars. He had rowed before, but never on a ship like this. After a dozen strokes, he got into the same rhythm as the others. Battle cries sounded from the Vikings who were on their way ashore, and soon shouts from the natives could also be heard. Marcus did not understand what they were calling but assumed they were as scared as he had been himself. As he was. The church bell rang even faster. Marcus sat with his back towards land and could not see what happened on the beach. He tried to pull his shoulders and neck under the shield, but for each new stroke, he had to stretch his arms forward, exposing his neck. He hoped the Irish did not have bows.

Not daring to look to the side when they began to row up the river, he concentrated on his rowing when they passed the places where the Northmen and Irish fought. The current became more potent, and they had to use more force for each new stroke at the oars. The shield weighed on him, and sweat ran down his forehead. When the first rays from the morning sun found his face, he wondered how far it was to the monastery.

An arrow skidded off the shield hanging on the back of the man in front of him and bounced into the river. The next arrow drilled into the wood inside the railing on the starboard side, killing all hope that the Irish had no bows. Marcus tried to pull his neck and head into the weapon shirt as he stared at the vibrating shaft with the grey feathers. Without breathing, he took two new strokes on oars while tensing every muscle in his body, waiting for the first arrow to penetrate his skin. Every moment was suffering. Every strain of the muscles dreadful.

The effort made him gasp for breath. The sound he made way too loud. He could just as well stand up and yell challenges to the Irish. Everything knotted in his body. He failed to take the next few strokes.

He felt a hand on his shoulder and gazed up at Magnus Trygg. His face gentle, his voice calm. 'Calm down, boy. And we will get out of here faster.'

It sounded so easy when Trygg said it but felt so wrong to do it. Marcus found solace in his words and glanced up at their leader. Trygg stood straight and unaffected in the middle of the ship as if no arrow in the world could hit him. Marcus gritted his teeth, stretched out his arms, and took the next stroke. One more. Then another. He fell back into the rhythm.

Suddenly it went quiet again.

They had passed.

The contrasts from the sea to the river were great. The river started wide but soon became narrower, and the wild forest around it crept ever closer to the boats. The vegetation along the river was dominated by small trees and shrubs, with dense branches bending over the water. All of which made it impossible to see further back. Archers could sit shoulder to shoulder along the entire river, and no one would know they were there until the arrows hit them. Nobody talked about it, but everyone knew it. The warriors who were not at the oars stared into the forest on the sides – eyes flickering from one shadow to the next. Now and then the woods opened up, and they could see buildings, cows and cultivated land. They saw no people and rowed on in silence. When the bushes and trees were back, the only sounds were the flowing water and the splashing of the oars. From the forest, they did not hear a sound, it was as if the woods held their breath as they passed.

Marcus did not know what was most exhausting. To row against the current, stroke by stroke, or waiting to get an arrow in the neck. He dared a whisper to the man sitting to his right.

'How far?'

The young man turned to face him. Marcus noticed he did not laugh at the question. These Northmen laughed at everything that could be perceived as cowardice or weakness.

'Far,' the man replied. 'We have to row all day. If we are not attacked, we may be able to get there before it gets completely dark.'

He stared ahead and spoke between the strokes. Marcus perceived no unkindness in his words. Perhaps the Northman was scared too? Marcus thought for a moment before he found the words to form a new question.

'Have you been here before?'

The man nodded. 'Yes. Twice. Three winters ago.'

He took a few more strokes on the oars. 'The first time went well. The monks had escaped and taken some valuables with them. There was no fight. But there were cups, goblets and crosses of silver and gold. Gemstones attached to books, and clothes of silk and linen. The loot was good that day.'

Marcus waited for him to continue, and his gaze turned to the forest. The fear threatened to get the better of him again. Even though his muscles went from aching to feeling completely numb, the fear weighed more on him than the rowing. It helped to listen to the Northman talking, and think of something else.

'The second time?' he asked.

From the corner of his eyes, he saw the Northman throw a quick glance at him. The compact Viking took a few more strokes before answering.

'These Irish are fighting well when they are fighting. They often fight each other and fail to gather forces until we are back at sea after a raid. Yet even small groups of Irish can give us a hard fight. They attack out of nowhere and disappear again. Until a few years ago, they did not have any quality weapons, but they are better equipped now. And they are accurate with arrows and spears and show great courage in battle with a knife or axe when they have to.'

The Northman uttered a few words between each stroke. It made it easier for Marcus to understand what he said. He thought for a long while before he came around to answering the question.

'The second time did not end well. Maybe they knew we were coming. Several clans were gathered. A large group of Irishmen attacked us shortly after we left the ships. Many of us were injured. Some were killed, and we had to leave some behind. We lost one man in three in a short time, before we managed to escape down the river. There was no loot from that raid.'

Marcus regretted the question. So the Irish were skilled warriors, too. He clutched at the last straw.

'The monks, are they fighting well?'

The Northman laughed briefly, a single grunt.

'No, they are not. But it is often the monks who gather the clans for resistance in an area when the Irish petty kings are unable to agree with each other.'

Marcus rowed on in silence, letting his mind process what he heard. 'Will we get attacked on our way there?'

The Northman snorted. 'Of course.'

Marcus could not decide whether he should be terrified by what the Viking said, or reassured that he seemed completely relaxed when he said it.

'A lot of fighting, or a little fighting?' He felt like a frightened little child as soon as he said it.

'A lot, I think,' came the reply. Still no grunts or laughter.

'But we want to live?' The frightened child in him took over completely. The vocabulary and nuances of the Norse language all but disappeared. However, the Northman did not appear to have any problems understanding him.

'Some will probably live. Many will die. There is room for many in Valhall.'

Marcus had heard that Valhall was a kind of kingdom for the dead Vikings, but did not understand why they were so eager to get there.

'Do you want to die and go to Valhall?' he asked.

The Northman answered in a monotonous voice:

'It's a shame not to come to Valhall. Helheim is for the weak, the sick and women. Actually, I enjoy being alive. At least I did until we had to row up this horrible river.'

'What is Helheim?'

'Helheim is … No, not today. It's a long story, and I can't bear to spend my last day talking about Hel. Ask me again if we live when the sun rises again.'

Marcus did not ask more questions. As soon as he stopped talking, he felt pain in his shoulders at every stroke, and dark thoughts re-emerged. He imagined the Irish mustering to attack further up the river and began to think about how he would have defended the island against the Vikings, if he was their leader. The Irish were probably not as strong and combat-hardened as the Vikings, so a man-to-man melee would favour the invaders. The Irish had bows, but he had heard the crew say they were smaller and not as powerful as the Northmen's bows. In that case, skilled archers could kill some and injure others, but they could not let the enemy catch up and engage them in close combat. If he led such a force, he would attack unexpectedly with a few dozen men, fire some arrows, and withdraw. With more men, they could hide in the dense vegetation along the river, and ambush groups of Northmen who were chasing the archers.

Instead of one great battle, there would be several small ones, at the same time, in different places. Marcus felt stronger and more secure when he thought of leading the forces and having the power to fight back.

'What is your name, thrall?'

The question from the man by his side took him by surprise. Partly because he resumed the conversation, but also because he addressed him as a slave. Marcus felt uncomfortable.

'Marcus,' he replied hesitantly.

'What does that mean?'

'I do not know. I think it's from Mars.' It was even harder to speak another language when he did not know what to say.

'What is Mars?'

'The Roman god of battle.'

'You have to row more often if you are to become a god of battle. Maybe learn to hold an axe too.'

The last sentence made Marcus turn to the Northman. For the first time, both smiled. Mars – the god of war – in the small form of Marcus.

'What is your name?' Marcus dared to ask.

'Bjarn.'

'What is it?' Marcus asked as the Northman did.

'It means bear. Big bear.' Bjarn emphasised the word 'big'. Both laughed. Bjarn was admittedly broad-shouldered, but no taller than Marcus.

'The big bear and the god of war,' Bjarn summed it up, 'We will win the day!'

When Marcus turned his gaze back from Bjarn, he startled so hard he lost his grip on the oars. He stared into a series of sharp teeth, just a hand's breadth from his face. And under the teeth, two wild, protruding eyes. The white coloured by red lines, and a large, black hole in the middle. Marcus's left arm grabbed at the oar, which was being pulled towards the rail while the oar blade cut deep in the water. His gaze unable to let go of the eyes in front of him.

'The smallest wolf plays with the little bear on the last day,' Geir Galne said.

He grabbed Marcus's shoulders and pulled him up until Marcus half stood and half hung from the arms of the berserk. The crew cursed and shouted in frustration, and Marcus heard several insults he had never heard before. The loose oar created all sorts of problems for the oarsmen. The handle was pulled out of Marcus's grip and hit the man in front of him in the back. The oar blade bore into the riverbed, and the ship started to turn towards the shore on the starboard side. Geir Galne stared into Marcus's eyes, without blinking. Over the skull, he had the head and upper jaw of a wolf and the pelt hung down over his shoulders and upper body. Galne bared his teeth in tandem with the wolf's head. Marcus had never seen him like this before. The old berserk breathed shallow and fast, and the fists holding Marcus trembled.

'Do you have soil between your ears, half-jotunn?'

Magnus Trygg was furious and grabbed Geir Galne from behind. Galne let go of Marcus and grabbed for his knife. Trygg averted the threat by pushing Galne backwards, towards Marcus and the sea chest he sat on. The berserk fell on his back against the legs of the man behind Marcus.

'That's enough nonsense from you,' Trygg continued, apparently not caring that Galne tried to draw a knife at him. 'Have two of your men replace the youngsters. Get to the bow and keep a lookout.'

Trygg grabbed the oar and lifted the blade out of the water. One of the berserks was quick to take the oar and Marcus's position on the chest. Galne crawled forward. Marcus chose to go backwards, as far away from Geir Galne as possible. He pressed himself down between two berserks, who sat with their backs to their respective barrels. Everyone who was not manning the oars sat next to barrels, chests or railing for cover. Marcus did not want to stand out as an easy target for Irish arrows and followed suit. Only Magnus Trygg stood upright, four short steps in front of him.

'Galne!' The firmness of Trygg's voice made it unnecessary to shout. Two bulging eyes under a row of wolf teeth appeared between the shoulders of the foremost oarsmen.

'What?' shouted Galne, with raised eyebrows and astonishment in his voice. The nearest oarsmen grimaced and threw uneasy glances at the forest leaning over the river.

'Pick out a few more of your berserks to row. My men cannot fight after rowing all day. Make sure four of yours are manning the oars at all times.' Trygg still did not raise his voice, but his tone and body language discouraged any discussion.

Geir did not seem to notice.

'Berserks are fighters, not oarsmen!' His mouth closed firmly, with the look of an offended boy.

'You can row, or you can swim,' Magnus Trygg said, his voice calm. Almost as if he had no interest in what the berserks chose to do.

Galne stared at Trygg without saying a word. Trygg's men still rowed, staring straight ahead in total silence. There were half as many of Galne's berserks as of Trygg's men on board. How could Magnus Trygg be sure he held the upper hand? It seemed Galne was thinking the same thing. Finally, he shifted his gaze to the side and pointed out two of the berserks sitting next to the railing. Galne sank back, out of sight. The berserks replaced two of the oarsmen.

The silence descended over the ship again, and Marcus closed his eyes. A good legionary sleeps when he is not on duty his father used to say, mostly as an excuse for nodding off during the day, as soon as he saw an opportunity. Marcus wondered if the same rule applied to oarsmen.

Something told him it was essential to save energy.

Chapter 22: Disservice

The arrow sunk into the man's back. Groaning his arms went up, he pushed his stomach forward as if trying to get away from the arrow. Then he fell to his knees. His arms bent backwards in an attempt to reach the projectile but to no avail. A few heartbeats later, he fell forward. On the ground, the man writhed and coughed blood. Ulv held the bow as if he were still aiming.

'Are you coming?' asked Vass.

There came no answer.

'Ulv?'

Ulv came to himself and tore his eyes away from the man he had just killed. Nodding, he walked towards Vass. He should have taken the arrow with him, but he was unable to even bear the thought of pulling it out of the back of the man who lay face down in his own blood.

Vass stood with one foot on the chest of an Irishman who lay motionless on his back. The pitchfork still stuck in the man's body as Vass pulled on it. It revealed two holes in the villager's chest as it came out. The fight was over. Vass threw the pitchfork aside and picked up a sword and an axe. He looked at the fork with two tines and sighed.

'Nice weapon, but if I am to continue fighting three at a time, it may be wise not to challenge the goodwill of the gods.'

Vass shifted his gaze towards Ulv.

'And perhaps you should consider hitting more than one out of three shots?' he said, grinning.

'How can you smile and laugh at all this?' Ulv asked quietly.

A rare serious expression spread across Vass's face.

'What else can you do? The way I see it, you have only two choices. Either you can ponder all the times you have to make a choice that is not really a choice, or you can just accept you have no choice. For instance, the choice between killing or being killed is not a choice that is particularly healthy to ponder too much. You will end up like a fool sitting on your ass and rocking while you drool and mumble. You might as well accept one of the things the gods are trying to tell us. If you fight and live, then you deserve to live. And those who are dead do not blame you.'

Back came the smile, and he continued: 'Besides, life is much more fun for people who smile. Of that, I am sure!'

'You have spent too much time with Geir Galne,' Ulv replied, shaking his head.

'Possibly,' Vass said. 'I hoped you would find a hidden meaning there somewhere,' and with that, his widest grin came back. He turned in the direction where the four men came from and waved his sword: 'Come on. We have more choices to make.'

Once again, Ulv thought about how wise it really was to follow the daredevil. Then it struck him that he really had no choice. He shook his head once more and felt the corners of his mouth pull up into something feeling much like a smile.

The sounds of fighting grew louder as they moved between buildings with wattle walls and thatch roofs. They were heading east towards the part of town laying at the top of the slope above the river and pool. Here the circular houses were replaced with square ones, but the construction method was the same. It smelled of rubbish. Food scraps and other leftovers were dumped in piles near the buildings. The sounds of battle abated, as they came to an open area and saw a large group of warriors. Across the open space, against the rising sun, a wall of earth was visible between the houses.

Ulv and Vass had to stop to avoid being run down by two men crossing right in front of them. Their faces distorted masks of fear. Two Northmen ran after them. The villagers were dirty and bloody and bore no weapons. Running with unsteady steps, they did not stand a chance. Laughing, the warriors behind them knew that too. One of the warriors, one of Torgils's decorated men, closed the gap to his victim and buried the axe in the back of the helpless man.

Ulv turned away.

It was no longer a fight. It was a slaughter.

'Bring those prisoners here!'

Ulv turned towards the sound, relieved to be able to focus on something else. It was Torgils who shouted. He stood with Ragnar and a couple of other men. The warriors shaded for the sun with one hand and stared at the earth wall. The rest of the inhabitants of the small town had entrenched themselves within the ramparts in the corner to the east, on the hill above the pool. A couple of warriors made their way between the Northmen, and past Ulv and Vass. They pushed a young man and a woman in front of them.

Torgils stepped behind the woman, put his left arm around her neck and held a knife against her throat. Then he led her forward, closer to the earth wall. The warrior who held the young man followed.

Ulv's stomach ached again. He stared at the two youngsters being led forward towards the gate in the rampart. They were also his own age. Maybe even younger. He envisioned the girl's face. He had seen her clearly when she passed by. Streaks down her face where tears washed away dirt and blood. Her hair dark, as were her eyes. Her gaze blank, she seemed to fall forward with every step. This was not about killing or being killed. This girl was not dangerous. There was no reason for anything to happen to her.

'We have to do something,' he told Vass.

Vass gave him a sidelong glance. 'I was afraid you would say something like that.'

Ulv turned and studied the young bare-chested warrior. Dark drops of blood were scattered all over his upper body and face. He did not look like someone concerned with rescuing anyone on the enemy's side. Young girl or not. Vass stared straight ahead. For many heartbeats they stood like this, Ulv looking at Vass, Vass staring at Torgils and the prisoners.

'Let's go,' Vass said in the end.

They headed back to the small open space between the houses where they fought the four Irishmen. The dead bodies lay where they left them.

'Is it true you are marked by Loke?' Vass asked.

Ulv stared at him. He did not even know how to begin answering the question.

Vass bent down and began removing the shirt of the man whom Ulv had shot in the back. 'Let's get dressed.'

Ulv did the same with one of the other men lying on his back with two holes from the pitchfork in his chest.

'We need someone like Loke looking after us right now,' Vass said, slipping the shirt over his head.

'What do you have in mind?' Ulv asked, assuming he would not like the answer.

'We dress like Irishmen, run past our people and towards the gate in the rampage. Then we hope they will open the gate for us,' Vass replied, his face all serious.

Ulv stared at him open-mouthed. 'I think Loke has hit you in the head!'

'What is your suggestion then, Ulv, son of Loke?'

Ulv did not know if Vass was offended or if he was joking. Pondering their options, he put on the dirty wool trousers he just pulled off the Irishman who lay dead at his feet.

'What do we do when we get in?' he asked, glancing at Vass.

'We chop off the worm's head,' Vass replied as if it was obvious.

Ulv could not understand how they would get away with such an act. But he agreed that they had to get in there if they were to accomplish anything.

'What if we get in from the outside? From the slope by the pool, we sailed past. They probably wouldn't pay much attention to that side when all the attackers are gathered outside the gate here,' Ulv said.

'Let's try,' was the only reply Vass made, before heading for the river.

'Wait, let me see,' Ulv said. He looked Vass over from head to toe, before shaking his head. 'You do not look like you belong here. Your own, or their clothes, it does not matter. It is you they describe in the stories of the warriors from the north!'

'They may think so, but no one wants to be right,' Vass replied, rubbing some dirt on his face. He hid his blonde, long hair in the leather helmet of one of the Irishmen, and put it on his head.

They went back down to the river and climbed the slope towards the pool until they reached the rampart. From the inside, they heard men and women shouting and screaming in a language Ulv did not understand. Anger, fear and despair were still evident in the cries. He wondered if the boy and girl were dead by now. In any case, the Irish had not surrendered. The two climbed to the top of the rampart and risked a glance over the edge.

There were three large buildings and several smaller ones. The large buildings reminded of longhouses, but they were built like the other buildings in the village. There were dozens of people: children and youngsters, adults and the elderly, women and men. A short distance back where they came from, a small house stood close to the rampart. Ulv pointed and crawled back that way. Behind the building, they climbed over the rampart and down the other side. Ulv glanced around the corner, saw an opening and walked out between buildings and among villagers, with Vass following close behind.

Ulv kept looking out for someone who seemed like the leader. It struck him that he did not know what to do when they found him. They could not walk over to him and cut off his head, as Vass suggested. Then he noticed a man staring at him. A shiver went down his spine. He glanced at Vass. The

Dane looked like he did not have a single concern in the world, but his smile was barely visible. That made Ulv uneasy. Perhaps he just did not want to attract attention, but Ulv felt safer when his friend grinned. He tried not to think about what would happen if someone, just one, realised they had nothing to do there. Of course, that only made it worse. Soon it was all he could think about. Sweat trickled down his forehead. His stomach knotted. The ground moved. He reached out for Vass to steady himself. Vass turned his gaze towards him and took him by the arm, hissing:

'We'll find the leader. But what do we do then? That is for you and Loke to decide. Think about that. Nothing else. It does not matter that you look scared or feel bad. That is how it is for most people here. You blend in nicely.'

Ulv tried to do as Vass said. He tried to think. Instead, he felt all the people staring at him as he stared at the ground.

'Chin up!' whispered Vass as he elbowed Ulv in the side. Ulv raised his head. Forced himself to look directly at people. No one glared. All he saw were scared, dirty faces. He thought of the boy lying dead with an arrow in his back. Thought of the man he stabbed. And the old man he stabbed in the stomach. Marcus's father. He thought of Marcus. He thought about Father. A man bumped into him and said something in an annoyed tone.

'I'm sorry,' Ulv muttered before he thought about it. He moved on, hoping the man would not shout after him. Towards the top of the rampart, there was a ledge where the defenders could stand with spear or bow protected by the upper part of the mound. Archers stood on the ledges, most on the side of the gate to the west where Ulv and Vass came from. Where the Vikings were gathered outside. Women and children were gathered in a group to the east, farthest from the gate, towards the river mouth.

'There!' Vass said, and Ulv startled.

He shifted his gaze forward. They entered between two longhouses that stood and formed a wedge with the opening towards the gate in the rampart. There were a lot of men there, battle-ready men. Right in front of them stood three people: a monk; a tall man with a shield, sword and spear; and a small, fat man with barely any hair on his head. They gesticulated and discussed loudly, but Ulv did not understand what they were saying. A fourth man stood nearby but withdrew as Ulv and Vass approached.

'Be ready with the bow,' Vass said and continued with determined steps towards the three men.

They were just three man-lengths away. Ulv saw Vass put his hand on the sword. Did he really intend to behead the man! Ulv wanted to tell him to stop, wanted to hold him back, wanted to say they had to come up with something else. Saying nothing, the moment was soon gone. I'm dead, thought Ulv.

Vass closed in on the three men, with Ulv a few steps behind. The men became aware of Vass. They looked at him as if annoyed at being interrupted. Vass held the sword in his hand. Ulv saw the exact moment the warrior understood something was wrong. His eyes widened, and his hand went down to his sword. It was too late. With the sword ready, Vass grabbed the man and swung him around in one abrupt motion. The man fought back, but in the next moment, Vass held the sword against the man's throat and spoke in a cold voice:

'Steady. Easy now.' Then he said louder, 'Pull back! Pull away, or he's dead!'

Vass glanced at Ulv. Ulv picked up the bow and nocked an arrow. He raised the bow and aimed it back and forth at the nearest men. The monk and the fat man raised their hands and withdrew slowly.

'So?' Vass said, looking at Ulv. 'What now?'

Ulv stared at Vass. He had no solution. No solution, except the obvious. The truth. He waded in.

'The Jarl will kill you all.'

The fat man seemed to understand what Ulv said, and spoke to the Irishmen in their language. The men reacted with angry shouts, and Vass stared at Ulv with raised eyebrows and a half-open mouth. Ulv continued:

'The Jarl will kill you all if you do not surrender.'

The exclamations were still angry, if not as strong.

'The Jarl will kill you all if you do not surrender and swear allegiance to Odin the Allfather.'

This time the shouts were at least as angry as the first time.

Vass glanced at Ulv and said in a sarcastic tone: 'This is going exactly as planned!'

Ulv shrugged. The warrior held by Vass spoke, and the area went quiet. After a few moments the men around started muttering.

'What did he say?' Ulv asked, glancing at Vass out of the corner of his eye as he continued to point his bow at the Irishmen.

'He said the blue berries in the forest are poisonous at this time of year,' Vass replied.

Ulv turned to him, open-mouthed.

'I do not know their language any better than you, Ulv! I have no idea!' Vass continued.

Ulv could not tell if Vass was exasperated or if he was just scared. It would be natural if he was afraid. It was natural to be terrified. Ulv was beyond that point. He was empty. He had given up. Then the fat man said:

'We want your promise the women and children will go free.'

To Ulv's great surprise, the man looked at him. Ulv did not understand. Did they think he decided? Did they think he was in a position promise something like that, that his words could tip the scales? Vass whispered through clenched teeth:

'Anything, Ulv. Promise anything.'

Ulv did not like it. Not at all. He made up his mind before hope took him. With hope, he would have taken the easy way out:

'I can't promise anyone will go, but I promise that those who turn to Odin and the åsatru, will live.'

He hoped it was true. He hoped Aud would seize the opportunity. Geir Galne had said she wanted to spread their faith to the people on the Green Isle.

The fat man translated, and the men began to discuss.

Vass said aloud, 'This man is going out with us anyway!'

Vass led the man out the gate. Ulv went backwards, with the bow aimed at the Irish.

'What is this?' asked Torgils when they came close enough to be able to talk to the warriors, who had gathered some distance from the rampart.

Behind Torgils stood Aud and Ragnar. Vass gazed at Ulv.

'This is their leader. I …' Ulv did not know how to proceed. He had not planned any further. He got the feeling Torgils would not be happy with the promises he had made.

'Yes? Spit it out, boy!' continued Torgils.

Ulv plunged in once more. Like a man on a cliff who does not know if he hits the water or the rocks below. He fixed his eyes on Aud, who stood a little further behind. 'I said those who surrendered to Odin would be allowed to live. If they came out without weapons and without resistance.'

Torgils said nothing but stared at Ulv. Ragnar spoke to the Irishman, who was still standing with Vass's sword against his neck. The man nodded and answered briefly. Ragnar glanced at Torgils.

'He confirms what the boy is saying.'

Torgils did not look happy. Not at all. He shifted his gaze from Ragnar to the Irishman, to Ulv and towards the rampart. Aud went to Torgils's side and whispered something in his ear. Torgils kept the dissatisfied grimace, but when Aud finished he looked at the Irishman and spoke.

'It is a deal. Those who convert to the åsatru will live.'

No one needed to hear what would happen to the others. Torgils turned his gaze to Ragnar.

'Tell him he can inform his men it's a deal. That they can come out, without weapons.'

Ulv took a deep breath. It felt like a long time ago.

Chapter 23: Blackwater

'Halfway there,' Bjarn had said when the ships left Boyne and continued up a narrower river that the Northmen called Blackwater. The Irish had not offered any resistance since they crossed the estuary. Marcus was tired after three sessions at the oars. Making it worse, some places they had to pull the ship over shallow sections. It had taken its toll on the whole crew. The sun hung low in the south-west, and most of the time, they rowed in the shade from the dense vegetation hanging over the river. Marcus found his place between the barrels in the back of the ship and sat eating some dried fish and a ripe apple. The wet clothes did not bother him while rowing, but he soon became cold when he sat still.

A sound from the north bank made him stop chewing and look up. Somehow, he knew what the sound was, but he could not comprehend what it meant. A heartbeat later, the sound grew louder, and Marcus did no longer doubt. It was the crackling sound of the trunk of a tree being felled. If trees were felled, there had to be people here. If there were people here, they were in danger. His brain reached the conclusion at the same time as his eyes saw the tree falling just in front of the mast. Everything became chaos. The ship cracked under the weight of the tree. Screams of pain from those hit were mingled with shouts and commands. Marcus heard two sharp thuds as two arrows drilled into the wood of the ship. Then there were two short thumps, from arrows piercing human bodies. More cries of pain.

'Out! Out!'

Marcus did not know who gave the order. Geir Galne roared something incomprehensible and jumped into the river on the same side as the tree had fallen. The berserks did as their leader. The oarsmen let go of the oars, grabbed their weapons and followed. Four men did not leave the boat. One of them was Bjarn. He sat completely still with his back to the ship's chest. An arrow protruded from the left side of his chest.

Marcus grabbed the axe but left the shield laying and jumped into the river. The ship glided downstream, and towards the riverbank as the tree got stuck in the vegetation on the north side. He took hold of the branches from the felled tree and pulled himself towards land, a bit further down than the others. To his right, men from Kjetil Korte's ship were also going ashore a half-hundred steps downstream. Marcus feared Kjetil more than any Irishman, so he climbed up the riverbank, crawled through the dense vegetation, and began to run uphill. Towards the sounds of struggle.

The first Irishman he met was dead, struck by a sharp blow to the neck and shoulder. The young man clutched a long knife in his hand. A bow lay on the ground not far away. Marcus considered for a moment whether he should take the bow with him, but rejected it. In a fight, he would be cut down before he could figure out how to use it to effect.

Shapes moved between the trees both in front of him and to the left. Marcus recognised the Northmen's battle cries, which he had heard when his own village was attacked. Many shouted 'Tyr!', others 'Odin owns you all!' The words stung him with a sharp fear every time. He heard the sound of metal against metal, metal hitting wood, and metal hitting flesh. Men screamed in pain and fear. The sounds came from many places at once, as if groups of men were fighting all around him. Sigurd Jarl's ship had been in front of them. If they were in battle, there would be three dozen Northmen further up. He took a firm grip of the axe, spat some dried fish still in his mouth from his meal on the ship and began to run up along the river.

An arrow flew past at an arm's length distance. Someone shouted. Marcus passed a small group of men in battle but ran on without finding out who they were. Something moved right in front of him. He lifted the axe with both hands on the wooden shaft. A man stood wide-legged in front of him. The man chopped his axe down against Marcus's head as if to split him like a log. The axe shafts collided; a sharp pain shot through Marcus's arms. He reacted quickly enough to block the blow, but made no attempt to stop. He hit the man squarely. They both fell. The man landed on his back, with Marcus on top. Marcus still held the axe with both hands, and he drove the shaft against the man's head.

A dull thump sounded, and all resistance ceased. Marcus got to his feet and ran on. He had no idea who the man was, whether he was Irish or Northman. It did not matter. He ran between trees, jumped over undergrowth, ducked under branches and veered away whenever he saw someone in front of him. All the while, he heard the sound of someone pursuing him, closer and closer. His heart thumped, and his breath wheezed.

'You!'

The voice made him shiver.

He turned his head and saw what he knew he would see. Kjetil Korte was chasing him. He held the sword in his right hand as he ran, but wore no shield or helmet. Marcus entertained no doubts as to who was the Northman's target. He dropped the axe, so he could move faster between the trees. He heard the trampling, breathing and the short insults Kjetil shouted at him as they ran. Kjetil came closer. Marcus could almost feel the breath on his neck and the sword in his back. He envisioned the Irishman who had been slashed between shoulder and neck.

Marcus threw himself on the ground and curled up with his back in the air. He felt the expected blow to the lower back, as Kjetil's leg hit him. The massive warrior stumbled over him and landed hard on the ground between roots and trees. Marcus jumped to his feet and went over to Kjetil, who lay on his back. Kjetil stared at him with wide eyes and creased forehead. He opened his mouth to say something, but Marcus did not wait to hear what the Northman had on his mind.

He stomped down with his heel against Kjetil's face. Something gave way. Kjetil growled and clutched at his face. Blood poured forward between his fingers, above, below and on the side of his large hands. Marcus calmly picked up Kjetil's sword and glanced at him once more. Kjetil was silent. Their eyes met. No word was spoken between them. There was no need.

Marcus turned away and started running. With Kjetil's sword in hand.

Chapter 24: Volve

Ulv stared at the inhabitants of Dyflin, who were lined up in a row. Those in the front were told to undress. Soon they stood waiting, naked. Waiting to be led around the corner of the building and away. Those who had been taken away did not return. An elderly man stood first in line. He was hunch-backed and seemed to have too much skin. As if the rest of him had withered away while the skin still had the same size. He was pale and thin. Still, he held his head high. Staring straight ahead, he clenched and unclenched his fists. Clenched and unclenched. Behind him stood a young woman. Just as naked. She tried to cover herself as best she could with her arms. Tears streamed down her round face, but she made no sound. She stared at the ground and trembled.

A little further back stood the young man who had pulled away when Vass snuck in and put the sword to the neck of the leader of the village. He met Ulv's eyes, but Ulv looked away. He could not keep his eyes off the girl and the old man.

This was his work. Once more, nausea crept up. If this was the feeling of saving someone, then he would never do it again. He missed Sigurd Jarl and Magnus Trygg. He even missed Kjetil Korte. They were brutal Vikings, but not like this. This was something else. These poor people were degraded.

A warrior came to fetch the old man. Ulv did not want to know what happened on the other side of the house. Still, he was unable to do anything but follow. The old man kept his head high.

Ulv glanced around before slipping between a couple of buildings where the row of villagers stood. He hurried in the door of an elongated house and crept up against the back wall. The roof arched far down on this side, so he got down on his knees to look under it. From there he saw through the braided branches the walls were made of. Outside, Aud stood waiting. She wore her green silk dress. The silver ribbon over her forehead, the jewellery, the rings and the belt with the gilded buckle were also in place. Over this, she wore a white apron smeared with red stains. Her long reddish hair hung loose.

She was a beautiful woman and a horrible sight.

The warrior led the old man in front of Aud. On a small table, she kept a trough and a brush, and a wooden figure representing the one-eyed Odin. The brush was of the same type that she used for the blot on Sanday. Aud dipped the brush in the trough and splashed blood on the naked old man. Her voice was hoarse.

'If you accept åsatru and renounce Kvitekrist and other false gods, repeat these words after me.'

She waited while the man blinked and wiped the blood from his eyes.

'I acknowledge Odin the Allfather as Lord of all gods.

In Åsgård as in all worlds.

Odin, son of Bor and Bestla, brother of Vilje and Ve,

father of Balder, Hod, Hermod and Tor,

is my god from now until the last night of my life.

To Odin who sacrificed his eye for wisdom,

and himself to himself, I bestow my life and livelihood.

To Odin and his brothers and sisters, children and kin, my life shall belong.'

The old man stuttered and stammered in the foreign language, and Aud had to repeat the individual parts several times before he could complete the verse. In the meantime, Aud continued to splash blood on him. Ulv held his breath as he stared between the braided branches in the wall. Then Aud nodded to the man and showed with an outstretched arm that he could move on. The warrior who had been waiting with Aud took the man by the arm and led him towards a cluster of buildings closer to the river. The warrior glanced back at Aud as they walked and Aud gave him a short nod. The Viking repeated the movement as confirmation and continued with the man. The old man's fists were clenched.

The girl gave up trying to cover herself. Tears made white streaks down her bloody cheeks. Still, she managed to say the verse with surprising clarity:

'To Ohdin, okay his brotters okay sisters ...'

'Children and kin, my life shall belong,' Aud repeated the last words.

'... children okay kin ..., my life shell belong,' the girl concluded.

Ulv wondered how the words the girl did not understand could have any meaning for the gods. He shook his head.

Aud nodded and signalled for the girl to leave. The warrior took her by the arm and led her away. He turned and looked back at Aud.

Aud turned her head slowly. First to the left, then to the right.

The man nodded and turned again. Thoughts raced through Ulv's mind. *Did that mean what he thought it did? Why?* He had to find out what they would do to the girl. About to follow the warrior and the girl, he saw the young man he had recognised, being led around the corner. The man had tousled black hair and a friendly face if one disregarded his stern eyes. They stared straight at Ulv.

His heart skipped a beat. *Could the young man see him?* Ulv pulled back and walked out the door. He followed the outside wall until he was able to look around the corner and saw the warrior who had followed the girl walking between the buildings on his way back. Ulv crept on and moved between two houses. On the other side of these, he expected to find the girl. He crept up to the last corner. His heartbeat pounded in his ears.

It was already too late. Ulv could not take in what he saw behind the cluster of small houses. He turned and walked away. Tears ran down his face. Quiet, heavy tears. Just like the girl had cried.

She would never cry again.

*

Ulv stared blankly in front of him, not noticing the last rays of sunlight reflecting on the surface of the river Liffey. He did not know how long he had been sitting there. His sleeves were wet from wiping tears. After wiping them away, he decided enough was enough. He could not sit there, crying like a child. Then the tears came back.

The river lured. Would it be difficult to drown? Would he be able to do it, or would a part of him fight back and strive for the surface?

He would not even manage to do that right.

A figure appeared where the glow from the sun turned into dark water against the shore on the other side. Ulv got up. Took up the bow and an arrow. Nocking the arrow, his eyes scanned the river. The figure climbed up on the bank. It was one of the Irishmen. It would be a catastrophe if the man got away and alerted the clans about the attack. They were not ready for another fight now. Ulv aimed at the man as he got to his feet on the grass. It was not an easy shot, but Ulv kept calm. He was confident of hitting. He had the confidence he lacked earlier that day.

He was calm and composed. Cold.

The black hair stuck wetly to the man's head. Ulv adjusted for distance, wind, and altitude. He took a calm breath and let the air out slowly. The man turned. Even at this distance, Ulv recognised the stern narrowed eyes. Their eyes met. Ulv still held his breath. The time was right.

Ulv lowered his bow and sat down again.

Chapter 25: Aftermath

Vass and Ulv had found an empty house in Dyflin. Now they sat in front of the fire and spoke softly. Vass had found a small keg of beer, and they both nursed a drinking horn as they leaned towards the heat. It was warm, but Ulv was cold.

Vass shifted in his seat, and Ulv could feel his sidelong glance. 'You did more for the people of this city than anyone else here today.'

'Yes, because of me, they did not get the chance to fight, but were slaughtered like lame cows,' Ulv replied, looking down at the mud floor.

'Many were allowed to live,' countered Vass, who once again stared into the flames. 'More people would have died if it were not for you. Count your victories,' the berserk continued. 'Or have you become spoiled by victories?' Vass smiled and threw Ulv another sidelong glance.

'Oh, shut up!' Ulv replied.

He could not cope with the berserk's ridiculous rosy view of life. Not now. Ulv wanted to sink into darkness. Not that it was difficult. He felt like being at the bottom of a shaft beginning in the realm of the dead with Hel. From there it continued downward for several days. Where Ulv now was, it was not dark. It was the place where darkness took from. He remembered the story of Loke's punishment. He wondered if Loke had been worse off when he was bound by his son's intestines, unable not move, and the venom of a worm dripped down on him. At least Loke had Sigyn with him. Sigyn held a cup over him and prevented the poison from dripping on to his face. When the cup filled and Sigyn went to empty it, the poison dripped on him. That's how Ulv felt. As if poison dripped down on his head. He wished he could create earthquakes, as Loke did when he writhed in pain. That, someone, would suffer for his pain.

He did not make earthquakes, nor did he have anyone like Sigyn.

Vass got up. It was as if he knew where Ulv's thoughts had taken him. 'I can tell you are occupied feeling sorry for yourself,' he sighed.

Ulv looked up at him. Vass had in a short time become the closest Ulv had to a friend. He did not want Vass to leave. He did not want to sit there alone.

'Wait,' he said quietly.

Ulv turned his face towards the flames again but felt the gaze from Vass who still stood there.

'Tell me something,' he said.

Vass sat down. For a moment they were both silent.

'Something about yourself,' Ulv said more firmly and glanced at Vass.

For a long quiet moment, Vass stared into the fire. 'That wouldn't be much fun. But I can tell a story about Geir Galne,' Vass smiled. 'It will give you something else to think about!'

It was dark outside. Vass sat whittling what looked like a miniature pitchfork, with two spikes. At the same time, he told stories about Geir Galne, other berserks, warriors and gods. Ulv listened, drank beer, and warmed himself by the fire. As the evening wore on, the cold gradually let go of him. From outside, they heard singing and howling from feast-minded Vikings in other parts of the village. Some close, others further away.

Ulv would rather stay in the small house. The melancholy did not completely let go, but he also entertained feelings he had not known for a long time. A sense of fitting in, of belonging, of camaraderie. A feeling the world was almost normal. The fact he was warm, full, and a little tipsy from the beer did not hurt either. Ulv dragged himself over to one of the benches next to the wall. He lay there listening to Vass. The young Dane was in the middle of a detailed description of Tor's fishing trip with Hyme the jotunn, where Tor fitted an ox head to the hook and caught the Midgard Serpent. Ulv knew the story well.

He closed his eyes. As Vass's words became more distant, Ulv thought about Marcus. Suddenly he was back in the burning house with the merchant's son by his side. Together they fought their way out. They chopped at the door with the smoke heavy around and flames licking at them. Ulv opened his eyes again, and was relieved the wall he stared at was not compact, but made of wicker. The words from Vass's tale reached him anew, and Ulv focused on Thor and the Midgard Serpent until his eyes slid shut and the world disappeared.

*

The next day, Ulv was put to work. The Vikings meant to stay for the winter, so there was a lot to do. First of all, the surrounding defences had to be improved. From the morning on, Ulv helped dig the ramparts. Others were sent to cut timber for pointed poles and palisades. It was hard work, but Ulv enjoyed feeling part of the community. He also saw some of the Irish working with enthusiasm. Ulv was relieved to see life seemed to go on for them. He allowed himself to think that several of them might not have been there today if it had not been for him. The thought brought a smile to his face, but only for a heartbeat or two. Other thoughts lurked in the back of his mind, as did the image of a young girl's tears. Ulv tried to push the memories away, bent his back and mirrored the efforts of the new recruits.

During the breaks, they ate well. There had been some cattle in the village and nearby fields, and the Northmen indulged in meat for their meals. Ulv did not miss the cold porridge.

After the first break, Ulv met Vass again, as they were dispatched to collect logs that were floated downstream and amassed in the pool on the south side of the village. On their way down to the river, the pair passed some of Torgils's housecarls. The well-equipped veterans went quiet when they recognised Vass and Ulv, and followed the young men with their eyes. One of the warriors, a broad-shouldered man with brown hair in a ponytail and a full beard adorned with rings, took a few steps closer. Vass did not seem to care. He wore a half-hearted smile and spoke calmly to Ulv:

'Later, when the work is over, we should practise. You need a little more weapons training, considering all the trouble you drag us into all the time.'

Ulv glanced at the warriors but shifted his gaze to Vass when the comment sank in. Vass could not in all seriousness mean Ulv was the one who got them into trouble? He saw Vass glance at him from the corner of his eyes, but otherwise, the Dane gave no sign he was joking. Nor gave him any sign to care about the Vikings who now stood perhaps twenty steps away and stared. The warrior with the ponytail shouted:

'Are you looking for slaves you can play with, Ass?'

Vass threw only a brief glance at the man and gave no indication that the wordplay on his name bothered him. He just kept on strolling while talking to Ulv.

'I can teach you a few tricks. And you're quick. I need to practise fighting someone faster than me. Usually, I'm the one with the speed advantage.'

Ulv looked at the man who had been shouting. He resembled a boy teasing his big brother, now unsure of whether he hoped to be ignored or get his full attention. Ulv shifted his gaze to Vass again.

'Not very talkative today?' continued the berserk.

Ulv shook his head.

'We can practise later. But what was that about?' Ulv nodded towards the warriors as they passed.

'Oh, that,' Vass replied as if he already had forgotten the man who just tried to offend him. 'It was just a little boy upset he lost his toy.'

Ulv looked at him questioningly, but it was clear Vass had no intention saying more on the matter.

There was already some timber in the deep pool. Half a dozen of the thickest logs were tied together at the ends to form a barrier across the river just downstream from the pool. On the riverbank by the barrier, several Vikings gathered and shouted loudly. Ulv first thought there was an argument brewing before he discovered that the men were smiling and laughing. One of the men picked up speed and began to jump on the timber – from log to log floating in the river by the barrier. Of course. The Northmen had invented another game.

It was their custom to compete against each other in every conceivable exercise that would measure strength, agility, speed, courage or other qualities. From early childhood, they strove to assert themselves in such sports as climbing, wrestling, swimming and running. Now they had found a new challenge, and the first participant was already halfway across the river. But that was as far as he got. A larger gap appeared between two of the logs, and the man tried to compensate by putting more force into the jump. It did not work. The log went under and the Northman plunged into the water, drawing wild cheers from the onlookers.

Ulv noticed that Ragnar also was present, sitting on the slope with a smile on his face. He reminded Ulv of an old grandfather who enjoyed watching his grandchildren play. Many of the Northmen gathered were his men. Several tried the challenge, but none was successful. Some were too heavy and gradually sank further down. Others ran out of logs and had to choose between sinking with the log or jumping into the water. Every splash and failure was followed by loud cheers and laughter. Ulv briefly considered trying, but decided against it. He had no desire to make a fool of himself in front of Ragnar's experienced warriors.

'Ulv!' Ragnar shouted and waved him over.

Ulv was both happy and surprised the old warrior remembered his name. He tried not to seem too eager as he hurried over. Ragnar signalled for him to sit, and Ulv obeyed as he saw Vass getting ready to challenge the logs. Vass chose a new, and of course, more daring approach. Standing by the water's edge, he retreated several steps before he set off towards the opposite bank. Instead of stepping hard on the logs, he opted for quick, light steps. The first part went like a breeze, and in an instant, he was halfway across the river. The speed became a little slower, but he had only a quarter left. Then, he was in trouble. He miscalculated, lost his balance and veered to the left. Still, he kept running. Almost there.

And entirely out of control. He lunged forward, reaching for the riverbank.

And landed on his stomach, an arm's length from land, to the biggest splash of the day. The cheers rose. The spectators laughed, pointed and patted each other on the back.

'Are you going to give it a try?' Ragnar asked, looking out over the river.

Ulv turned towards the Dane, wondering if the old man was joking with him. Ragnar shifted his gaze to Ulv and answered the question that had not been asked.

'I think you might have a chance.'

Ulv did not quite know what to say, so he remained silent as he watched Vass swim back and climb ashore. Soaked, but with the familiar smile on his face.

'You are agile,' Ragnar continued, 'and lighter than the warriors down there.'

A fair point.

'And I'll tell you how to avoid the mistake others have made,' Ragnar said.

Ulv felt the excitement at the thought. Ragnar pointed to the logs on the river.

'You have to look further ahead. Always look beyond what you think is necessary. You must have the entire route planned from start to finish. And then, you have to look further ahead than you think. If you look straight down at where to put your feet, you will have too little time. Looking ahead, you will still remember enough to put your foot right in the next step, and the next, and the next.'

Ragnar's eyes fell on Ulv again as if to emphasise the point. 'Always look further ahead, Ulv. Force yourself to plan several moves ahead. Every move, until you're over. Until you have won.'

Ulv was not sure if the old fox still talked about crossing the river.

Ulv studied the river and the logs, planning which logs he could step on and which ones he should avoid. The smallest logs would not even hold his weight. A couple of other warriors tried. The logs did not move much, so he could make a plan. He imagined where he was going to step and that he made it over to the other side. He *felt* ready. Went through the route again. He *was* ready.

Ulv got up and went down to the riverbank where Vass came to meet him. He stopped, smiled and wished Ulv good luck. His determination was apparently visible.

Four steps from the water he stopped and took a deep breath. Then, he set off in a half run. Not a wild sprint like most of the others. Ulv stepped on the first logs and was on his way. His gaze fixed a man's length further forward. It was easy. It worked! Soon halfway. He stuck to the plan and avoided the smaller logs. The pace was steady.

But then, all of a sudden, he found himself in trouble. One of the logs in his route had drifted off, forcing him to improvise. He stepped down on one of the smaller logs, but put little weight on his foot. Just a half step to keep his balance, but enough for his low-cut leather boot to fill with water. He compensated by stepping harder on the next log. Was it stable enough for it to work? He got to the next one. Just a few more man-lengths. He no longer had control over the plan or the route, and did not manage to look ahead either. Looking down, his steps became too short and he shuffled his feet as best he could. He was entirely out of balance. He would fall!

Ulv stumbled. And fell.

In wet sand.

He was over. He had done it. On the other side, it was all quiet. Then he heard a roar of joy. It started with Vass's voice, then others followed.

Behind the group of warriors on the riverbank, Ragnar was smiling and nodding to Ulv.

Further up the slope, several more onlookers stood. They had probably heard the commotion and had come to see what was going on. Ulv smiled as he had not done for a long time.

Well over on the other side, the warriors patted him on the back. They smiled and shook their heads. Ulv met Vass's gaze, and they both grinned.

For the first time, Vass's grin did not match his own.

Chapter 26: Honour

Marcus found the Jarl's ship on the shore. He could not see any damage to the vessel or any injured or dead men on board, so he assumed they had disembarked on their own accord. A battle had been fought on the shore, leaving a dozen Irishmen and about half as many Northmen scattered around him. The Irish had been waiting for the invaders, and welcomed them with arrows and spears.

Marcus turned towards the sounds of combat further into the forest, where there seemed to be a major skirmish. He walked calmly towards the battle as if the sword had bestowed upon him courage he had never known. He passed several dead and wounded from both sides.

'Boy!'

The word sounded like a grunt. Marcus stopped. The heathens usually called him 'thrall' or 'pup'. But on rare occasions, someone said 'boy'. It was probably the nicest name he had. Perhaps that was why he stopped.

A man lay with his back to a tree, half concealed by bushes and undergrowth. A spear shaft protruded from the left side of his abdomen. Marcus lifted his gaze to the unkempt beard and the black hair that was plastered to the pale skin with sweat, and concluded that this man would soon be dead.

'Sigurd Jarl,' Marcus nodded.

The Jarl responded with a grunt. He stretched his arm towards Marcus but moaned and lowered it again.

'Help me to my feet, boy!'

Marcus walked over to the Jarl and squatted down beside him. He examined his head, arms, body, and legs, as his father had taught him. He found several minor injuries, but nothing that gave cause for immediate concern. Except for the spear in the abdomen.

'Pull it out and help me to my feet,' ordered the Jarl, without the usual conviction that follows half a life of absolute authority.

'I can do that, but that will make you die sooner,' Marcus replied. He did not mean to be so direct but did not know enough Norse words to soften the blow.

The Jarl glanced at Marcus again. 'Yes, you're probably right. I will not recover from this wound.'

Marcus nodded and sat down beside the Jarl. He wished he had wine or at least some water for the man. That was what one was supposed to do when someone was dying – offer them something do drink. He looked apologetically at the old chieftain.

'Do not have wine. Not water.'

The Jarl produced a lopsided smile. 'It's fine. I do not think I will die from thirst anyway.' His smile widened; the Jarl seemingly pleased with his joke.

'How's the fight?' Marcus asked, pointing to the battle in front of them.

'Not great' the Jarl replied, 'our men are losing. They have joined forces with Magnus Trygg's men, but they are still losing ground. The fighting is much closer now, and I hear in their cries that they have lost control. Soon, they will retreat to the ship. There is no reason for everyone to die here in the forest.'

'I thought Northmen preferred to die in battle.' Ulv had told Marcus it was an honour to die fighting, but no honour in fleeing the battlefield.

'No, we would rather live,' the Jarl replied. 'But if we are going to die, it is best to die in battle. Only the weak die from disease and old age, and they will never sit at Odin's table in Valhall.'

Marcus nodded as he considered the words. The reasoning was simple and practical. Ahead, no more than twenty steps away, the fighting came ever nearer. One Northman fell, another struggled against three Irish at the same time.

'I am ready,' the Jarl said after a short while. 'Help me up and let me finish this.'

Marcus looked him in the eyes and nodded. The Jarl was ready. Marcus got up and grabbed one of the Jarl's arms with both of his, and braced his legs so as to be able to pull the heavy man to his feet.

'Wait,' the Jarl said, looking down at the spear shaft sticking out of his belly. 'It hurts a bit to move with this stick in my stomach. Pull it out first.' The understatement was obvious.

Marcus did as asked, and extracted the spear in a steady motion. The Jarl jerked and clenched his teeth in pain. He made some indefinable noises, a kind of rattle, while his face became even paler, almost green. Opening his eyes, he held out his arm again.

'Now, boy!'

With a heroic effort, the Jarl came to his feet and leaned on Marcus.

'Good,' the Jarl said.

He took a deep breath and shouted, louder than Marcus imagined he was capable of.

'Retreat! To the ships! Retreat!'

The men in front of them recognised the Jarl's voice. They reacted immediately, and with trained movements, they danced backwards in groups of three and four. One engaged the enemy, while the others retreated. Then the frontman withdrew while his comrade engaged the enemy.

As the Northmen passed them on their way to the ship, Marcus recognised some of their faces. He did not know them by name, except Arngrim, who had laughed so hard when Marcus had fumbled the axe. The warrior nodded to Marcus as he passed. To the right, Magnus Trygg was shouting something. Geir Galne was nowhere to be seen. Not as many as twenty Vikings remained, Marcus realised.

The Irish chased the invaders, until they discovered the Viking chieftain in his predicament. Soon, three dozen Irish, a few women among them, fanned out around them at a distance of about ten steps.

'Good,' the Jarl said for the second time. He aimed his spear at the Irish, and moved the tip in an arc, challenging and warning each of them.

'Use this instead,' Marcus said, and handed the Jarl the sword he took from Kjetil Korte.

The Jarl took the sword and studied it with admiration. 'A good blade, and one that I recognise. I bet there is a story to go with it, which I would love to hear!'

'I will tell you tomorrow,' Marcus replied. 'A little busy right now.'

'Very good,' Sigurd Jarl replied, just as dryly.

'Why do they stop here? Shouldn't they be fighting the others?' Marcus asked.

Some Irishmen pursued the Northmen towards the ships, but more than half stood around him and the Jarl.

'Do you want me to tell you why?' The Jarl gazed at the Irish waiting with drawn weapons.

'Freedom? Gold? Duty? Family?' Marcus said.

'All good reasons. But most important of all is honour. Honour and fame, and everything that comes with it. It is a great honour to defeat a Viking chieftain. These Irish are waiting because they have not decided who should get the honour of killing me.'

'How do they know you're a chief?'

The Jarl started laughing, but his face soon broke into a grimace. 'Why else would our strong warriors take such a fat old man on a raid?'

Marcus looked at the Jarl, and accepted his point. The chain mail armour and the ornate sword also revealed that this was an important man.

The Jarl continued. 'One of them will soon lose his patience. A young man, who sees an opportunity to improve his position in the clan. He's going to die. Then a couple more, preferably at the same time. If I still manage to lift the sword after defeating them, I reckon they will shoot some arrows to weaken me. Then, and only then, comes the experienced warrior, who will kill me and call himself king. The Irish have more kings than I have bones in my body.'

As if the Irish understood what he said, a young man stormed forward with an axe raised. The Jarl took a step forward and parried with an effortless movement of his arm. The sword met the axe shaft on its way down, and the axe slid along the blade, harmlessly down and to the right of the Jarl. The old warrior drew his sword back in the same motion. In the next moment, the sharp edge cut into the unprotected belly of the Irishman. He sank to his knees, holding on to his stomach with bloody hands. Soon, he lay lifeless in a pond of blood.

Sigurd Jarl staggered and leaned so heavily on Marcus that he nearly fell over. The stain on the left side of the Jarl's stomach had grown, and blood seeped down his left thigh.

The Jarl could barely hold his head up, and he struggled to keep his grip on the sword. Marcus used all his strength to keep the Jarl upright as another Irishman charged them. He was better equipped, with a helmet, a shield, a heavy shirt and a shortsword.

The challenger advanced and thrust the sword against the Jarl's neck, as if he was killing a fish. The shortsword never came close. The Jarl parried and sent the blade spinning out of the Irishman's hands. In the next moment, he slashed against his adversary's unprotected left knee. There was an awful sound of iron against bone and cartilage, and the Irish howled in pain. But only for a moment, until the Jarl's sword found the side of the man's neck and brought him to silence.

Marcus lifted his gaze to see how the Irish reacted to the death of another of their young warriors. A tall and slender man with hollow cheeks and stern eyes stepped forward. He wore a tight-fitting tunic and high leather boots. An ornate handaxe hung at the right hip. He could not be more than thirty, but it was evident he enjoyed great respect. Calmly, he grabbed a spear from a nearby warrior, and weighed it in his hand.

Without further warning, he took three quick steps forward and threw the spear.

A moment later there was a dull crunch, as the heavy iron spearhead sunk into Sigurd Jarl's chest.

The Jarl jerked and fell dead to the ground.

Chapter 27: Price

'Why don't they just run away?'

Ulv and Vass relaxed with a horn of beer in front of the fireplace in the small, circular house. Ulv was tired and sore after a long day of working and sparring. Vass was not.

'The Irish?'

'Yes, they should be able to get away. They walk around freely,' Ulv continued, warming his free hand in front of the flames.

'I do not know, but I think there are several reasons. Perhaps they feel it is safer to stay, that it is better to spend the winter well fed inside the palisade than out in the woods or with poor relatives. Those who survived

Aud's ritual, have been treated fairly. Torgils has told them that the war is over and that we all can go back to living. Together.'

Vass shrugged and continued.

'Many Northmen and Danes were angered by Torgils's attempts at converting the Irish. Aud's rituals are cruel, but they might have pushed the survivors over to our side. Ragnar said that when people endure something horrible, they often try to explain it to themselves afterwards. They sacrificed a lot to please Odin and Torgils, so it has to mean something. Otherwise it was all for nothing.'

'But they had no choice!' Ulv said, annoyed.

'No, no real choice. But it can be easier to say to yourself that it was your choice, than admit you did not have the courage to stand up for yourself and your god,' Vass continued in a low voice. 'And while the sun moves over the sky, and they work and eat alongside us too, they are pulled further into it. Like a fish wriggling in the net just gets more and more stuck.'

They sat in silence and stared into the flames.

'According to Ragnar, we should not be surprised if some of them are more devoted to Odin than we are,' Vass said, and took a sip of the drinking horn.

'But some did run away,' Ulv replied.

'Yes, at least one young man got away. One of the other Irishmen said almost his entire family was killed in the attack, and his sister did not return after the ritual.'

Ulv said no more. He thought about the young girl with tears on blood-red cheeks.

*

Ulv lay on his back, trying to catch his breath. Vass had just given him a compelling demonstration of an alternative way to use the axe. He hooked the end of the axe blade behind Ulv's knee and pulled. Ulv's foot, on which he held most of his weight, disappeared, and he thumped hard to the ground. It was no joke sparring with the young berserk, but Ulv had already learned a lot.

'They're back,' someone shouted, and Ulv raised his head to look towards the source.

The older warrior continued. 'The Jarl and his men are back from the raid.'

Vass gave Ulv a hand and pulled him to his feet. Ulv brushed the mud from his trousers when he saw Geir Galne came strolling as only Geir Galne could. As if the whole world was his. Galne glanced at Vass.

'A barking dog always finds a yapping pup.' He spat the words as if they were poison.

'You have to sing with the birds you keep company,' Vass replied with a smile. Ulv was not sure what that meant.

'He who runs around with wolves learns to yowl,' Galne shot back.

Ulv was nowhere near understanding any of this.

Vass shook his head, patted Galne on the shoulder. 'Come, Ulv, let's find the ships and see if there's anything left of our equipment.'

It would be nice to swap the borrowed wool clothes for his own. But as soon as they started walking towards the ships, his stomach turned into a knot. Would Marcus be there? Was he all right? He hadn't thought much about Marcus lately. Too much had happened in his own life. Now, however, he was worried.

From the men they met on their way to the ships, they learned that the raid had not gone according to plan. They faced stronger opposition than anticipated, and neither Sigurd Jarl nor Magnus Trygg had returned. Trygg's ship was damaged and left for repairs at Glumra's camp by the Glyde, it's stores and equipment moved to other ships. Nothing was known about Marcus.

They arrived at the ships, and Ulv found his chest. When he rummaged around in it, his hope turned to disappointment. The trousers, the padded shirt and the old bow, were all gone. He found the tunic, the cloak, the stolen silver goblet and the leather purse with the arrowheads from Sanday. He was still searching through the chest when Vass spoke behind him.

'Finished?'

Ulv turned his head and found Vass looking at him questioningly. Vass had dressed in the clothes he threw off at Hoy. Ulv sighed and got up. He removed his woollen shirt, threw it on the chest and put on his tunic. He took the cloak, the mug and the leather purse with him, threw one last glance around, and nodded to Vass.

They headed back towards the open square in the middle of the village. Ulv hoped it was Marcus who had borrowed the equipment. If so, he would get it back as soon as he found him.

'PUUUUP!'

Ulv startled, and a shiver went down his back. He knew that voice, even though it was changed somehow. More nasal.

Ulv immediately realised the good times he had experienced over the last few days were over. Just like when you know that the nice summer day is over when you hear the crash of Thor's hammer, and the wind picks up.

Around them, everyone stopped talking and looked towards the sound. Ulv took a deep breath and turned. Kjetil stopped a few steps away from him. At least, he did not intend to strangle him there and then. Savour every one of your victories, Vass had advised him. The thought made Ulv smile. It was probably not wise. He studied Kjetil.

Kjetil had seen battle. That much was obvious. Most notable was his nose. Crooked, and flatter, somehow. Kjetil Korte had obviously taken a blow to his face. His eyes were angry but controlled. Ulv got a sinking feeling. This was not good. Mindless rage was bad enough, especially with a giant like Kjetil Korte. But this was worse. Ulv's smile disappeared as Kjetil stared at him without a word. What was he waiting for? The crowd drew closer around them. Kjetil wanted witnesses! This was a moment he wanted people to see. The sinking feeling in Ulv's gut did not improve.

A loose ring of people formed around Kjetil and Ulv. Vass stayed next to Ulv. Kjetil took his eyes off Ulv and glanced around at the gathered men. 'What is the punishment for a thrall who attacks a free man?'

'Death,' several voices around him replied. Some were Kjetil's men, but others said the same thing.

'And who is responsible for holding the thrall accountable for his crime?'

'The owner,' came the quick response, a little too quick, from several sides. From Kjetil's men.

Ulv understood where this was going. Marcus had attacked Kjetil. Had Marcus broken the giant's nose? It was almost too good to be true. Ulv had to cover his mouth to hide the smile pulling at the corners of his mouth. But the smile disappeared quickly. Where was Marcus, then? Ulv took his hand from his mouth. 'Where's Marcus?'

'The cowardly rat attacked me while I was down. Then he took my sword and ran! 'Kjetil answered with his new, more nasal voice.

'He's a thrall and a *niding*. He has been sentenced to death,' Kjetil continued, calm and controlled once more.

'You can punish the thrall when you find him,' Ulv replied, before he could think. It was a mistake. It sounded like indifference to what his thrall had done. The Northmen would not like that. That was not their way. You had to take responsibility. The men around him began to murmur to each other, some shook their heads, others stared angrily at Ulv.

Kjetil spoke again. 'Your thrall is your responsibility.'

The men nodded and agreed. Ulv had nothing to say. He should not have said anything earlier, either. The unpleasant feeling of having stepped right into a trap laid by Kjetil Korte intensified. Ulv never doubted that the giant could take his life whenever he wanted, but he had not imagined being outsmarted by the brute. Ulv did not know how to reply. Kjetil waited. He let the men around draw their own conclusion. When he spoke again, his tone dripped of mock solemnity:

'Would you say it is fair that the owner should be outlawed until he can hold his thrall responsible for the crime?' Kjetil let his gaze glide over the assembled men again. Several men nodded, and others shouted 'yes!' or 'fair!' or 'more than the boy deserves!'

Kjetil looked at Ulv, his face an expression of exaggerated regret as he spread his arms out wide. 'It does not look like we have a choice, boy. You must leave the village as an outlaw. When you bring your thrall back, so he can take his punishment, you are a free man once more. Until then, take the punishment for your thrall.'

'As you wish, flatnose,' Ulv muttered as he turned to leave. He said it a little too loudly. He heard fast feet and felt a hand grabbing for him. A large hand. Ulv looked over his shoulder. The indifferent expression on his face was genuine. Two of the men held Kjetil back.

'Not now,' one of the men hissed in Kjetil's ear. Kjetil only got hold of the arrows in Ulv's quiver. His face changed as Ulv studied him. The folds on his forehead disappeared, a smile spread across his now relaxed face:

'You will hardly have a use for these,' he said, breaking the arrows and throwing them away.

Ulv walked away with calm steps.

Vass came after him. For a while, they walked side by side in silence. Vass picked up an axe that leaned against a stack of wood and gave it to Ulv.

'You'll need this.'

Ulv accepted the axe and nodded. They went quiet again. There was not much to say. As they reached the outskirts of the village, Ulv stopped. A small road led to the west.

'Thank you, Vass,' Ulv said, and turned to his friend.

Vass nodded. 'Take care of yourself. I'll see you later.'

'Possibly,' Ulv replied. He tried to smile, but he could not hold it. The corner of his mouth started to tremble.

He turned and started walking.

Chapter 28: Lone wolf

Ulv followed the path inland. It struck him there was a greater chance of meeting people if he stuck to the road, so he cut off to the left and walked into the woods. Besides, he refused to show any fear or weakness at being thrown into the wilderness in a foreign land. Not even to himself. If he had felt alone before, it was nothing compared to what he would be facing. Just as well, he said to himself. If there was one thing he had learned lately, it was that he could not trust anyone else. So, why should he keep company with a bunch of brainless savages?

In a small clearing in the woods, he sat on a tuft of grass and took stock of his possessions. He had the water skin and some flatbread from the day before. In the belt pouch, there was flint and steel, a piece of rope, a handkerchief and the small pouch with the arrowheads from Sanday. The axe Vass had found lay by his side. And of course, he had his seax and the bow Ragnar had given him on the ship.

Ulv strung the bow, but was not strong enough to draw it all the way. It did not matter, seeing as he had no arrows. He would have to find some suitable branches for shafts, and convince a bird to surrender his feathers.

Fortunately, he wore his cloak, which would serve as a blanket on chilly nights. Apart from the clothes on his back, this was all. There was much work to do if he was to survive, and even more work if he was to have any sense of comfort. He shook his head and mumbled a rare request to the gods. Why had they helped him through the trials so far, only to let him die like an incompetent fool in the wilderness? Clearly, he was out of favour with the gods. Succumbing to the dark thoughts, he laid his cloak on the grass and threw himself down.

In his restless sleep, he dreamed of dark cellars, burning houses and huge warriors who hated him.

Ulv woke up with a gasp. In his dream, he had been drowning in ice-cold water. The relief from realising he had been dreaming vanished when he discovered he was wet all the same. It was raining. He got up, shook the water from the cloak and put it over his shoulders. Pulling the hood forward to cover his face, he went in search of shelter.

The day was coming to an end, and the light was fading. Ulv sought higher terrain in hope of finding a cave, or at least an overhang that would shield him from the downpour. His mood and his luck matched the grey weather. Come nightfall, he still had not found a suitable refuge. Eventually, he crawled under some low branches of an old tree.

Sitting with his back to the trunk, he folded his arms around his knees and pulled them tight against his chest. Wet and cold, he huddled there through the night. The afternoon nap meant it took a long time before he could sleep. Every time he dozed off, he would wake up trembling from cold and fear.

Sounds are always more frightening in the dark of night. Once, he was awakened by a wolf howling not far away. With his heart pounding like Thor's hammer, he pondered the end of this saga. Ulv's saga: 'The fool called Ulv endured his last days wet and cold in a forest. His body would be food for the animals from which he was named. The wolves that tore his tough flesh from his bones were happily unaware of the irony.'

'Ulv Wolf food' would never be more than a phrase in the sagas of the Northmen's raids to the islands in the west. The truth was even bleaker: of course, there would be no saga about him. There was nobody to learn of his fate or to tell the story of his demise. With that sobering thought, Ulv fell asleep.

He woke up when Father kicked him and uttered the words he had heard hundreds of times before: 'Rarely does the sleeping wolf get the steak.' Ulv was up before he realised it was another dream. He shook it off and noticed the sun rising. He thought of his father and knew that the old man would indeed kick him if he found him in this sorry state. Father was right. Matters would not improve by his sitting under a tree and feeling sorry for himself. Feeling wet and cold was a privilege only for the living. It was time to change the saga.

He needed to find water, food and shelter. Water would not be a problem in autumn in this terrain. A man could survive without food for ten days or more. Father had taught him that. But to avoid getting weak and careless, he required both food and water. He could hunt, and build traps. But first of all, he would have to find shelter to keep him warm and dry.

A stream of running water would be a good place to start. Running water was preferable to still, and more likely to be clean. If animals drank from a stream, it would be safe for him as well. Despite limited knowledge, he'd seen some plants he knew to be edible, but most were unfamiliar to him. Either way, finding a stream was his first objective. It should not be that difficult. Ulv glanced up at the sun as it broke through the clouds and walked off in that direction.

*

At the end of the day, Ulv was in fine spirits. He had found a suitable campsite by a hill, not far from a stream. No animals had drunk from it, but he explored the area upstream without finding anything that might foul the water. Still, he chose not to drink from it and contented himself with the little he found of fresh rainwater on leaves and in small puddles. He ate some berries and lichen. His most significant discovery, however, was a dead crow. Not that he wanted to eat an animal without knowing how it died, but the feathers could be used for the arrows. Crow feathers were probably not what a fletcher would choose, but they would have to suffice.

Ulv was happy with the campsite itself. The rock sloped inwards, so he would be protected from rain next to the rock wall. At least as long as the direction of the wind was favourable. Either way, it was better than nothing. He gathered some firewood for the campfire and was determined not to freeze during the night. With a bonfire burning under the rock wall, Ulv sat down and examined the arrowheads and crow feathers.

If he found wood for the shafts tomorrow, he would be able to make some arrows. With the arrows, he could go hunting. Ulv fastened the bowstring and drew the bow a few times. It had not become easier, and he decided to work on this challenge daily. He was eager to test the technique the previous owner of the bow used. Apparently, he could fire arrows faster if he learned the style of archery Ragnar's men had talked about.

From there, his thoughts wandered to Vass. Ulv was grateful for the time he had with his friend, and sad because it had been taken from him. He thought about their conversations, and about what he told Vass about himself. He picked up the shiny goblet he had stolen from the Jarl of Gaular and thought of the part of the story he had not told Vass. About how the story actually ended. How he had been on his way out with the mug in his belt pouch but turned when the thrall entered. He thought about how he fled further into the house and to the bedrooms at the back. The woman he met there, her eyes and how she studied him calmly without making a sound. She was neither surprised nor frightened. Ulv thought of how she distracted the Jarl when he came in to find dry clothes, how she turned the Jarl away from the dark corner where Ulv stood. She took the Jarl to bed with her, so that Ulv would get out.

This part of the story he had not been ready to share. He did not understand. Had it really happened? It seemed more like a dream, so unlikely, so vague in a way. But at the same time, so infinitely clear. Those eyes, he could never forget her eyes. He imagined the woman until he noticed that his eyelids slid closed again and again. He took the string off the bow and pushed it and the other equipment farther under the rock. Then he lay down where he sat, between the fire and the stone wall, and fell asleep.

*

Ulv awoke when the air was blown out of him.

He opened his eyes, sat up and pulled back in the same motion. It was dark. He could not breathe. A man stood over him with an evil grin, displaying a row of brown teeth. In his hand was a long knife. Ulv's seax. Behind him stood two other men. One held a bow, the other a spear. The man with the brown teeth said something to him. It sounded like a command. He kicked again. That was what had blown the air out of him: kicks from the ugly man. The man had a wrongness about him, just as one would expect from an evil madman. He had that expression in his eyes. That expression that told you there is no way to tell what he is capable of.

Ulv knew it anyway. Pain. Violence. Death.

There were two more men in the background. They picked up his things. The waterskin, the cloak, the belt pouch and the silver goblet. He only had his clothes left. Browntooth shouted. And kicked. Ulv could barely move, but he avoided the brunt of the attack. He took a deep breath, dizzy and in pain. His hands were cold, and searing pain burned his stomach. The man shouted again and gestured. What did he want? Browntooth turned his head to the side and said something. The two men in the background came closer and bent to grab Ulv. He tried to pull away, but there was no more room. They lifted him up.

Browntooth barked again, while staring at Ulv. Again, that evil grin with those brown teeth. The men began to pull at his clothes.

'What do you want?' Ulv cried.

Browntooth said something, glanced around at the other men and laughed. The band undressed him. One of the others had found Ulv's rope. A moment later, Ulv stood in his undergarments while the two ruffians held him. Browntooth put the knife to his throat and said something incomprehensible. He kept talking as he moved the blade down to Ulv's chest.

Then, he slowly inserted the tip of the knife into the skin and pulled it at an angle down the chest.

The knife cut through the skin, and blood began to flow. Ulv gasped in pain, but did not shout. He did not know why, but he was sure yelling and screaming would please this man. And the last thing Ulv wanted was to please him. Browntooth cut a gash from the other side as well, making a red cross over Ulv's chest.

The man with the rope shouted something as he stood by a tree a few steps away. Browntooth slammed his fist in Ulv's stomach. Ulv bent over, but the bandits did not let him fall to the ground. They pulled him towards the tree, while Browntooth studied Ulv's seax.

Browntooth said something to his band and left. The men holding Ulv placed him with his back to the tree, pulled his arms back and fastened the rope to his wrists.

Browntooth shouted from the woods. His words were incomprehensible, but his voice was laden with excitement. The men mumbled and dragged Ulv with them again.

Browntooth had found an even better tree. The appeal of this particular tree was the anthill underneath. Ulv was tied to the tree, with his bare feet well planted in the anthill.

There, bleeding, bruised and helpless, with ants crawling up his legs, they left him. To die. A slow, painful death.

Just as evil men wanted it.

Chapter 29: Amen

Marcus felt a peculiar sadness at the loss of the brave Jarl who had caused his father's death, abducted his sister and enslaved him.

He shifted his gaze from the Jarl to the tall Irishman who stood motionless. If he felt any joy in having killed the Viking chieftain, it did not show in his stern face.

Marcus stooped and seized the sword lying next to Sigurd Jarl. He held no illusions of faring better against the Irish champion than the Jarl had done. And Valhall was not for his kind.

Marcus placed the tip of his sword to the ground, kneeled and folded his hands over the hilt. He closed his eyes and began to pray.

'Pater Noster, qui es in caelis, sanctificetur nomen tuum …'

He hoped God, who saw everything and heard everything, would listen to his last prayer.

'Adveniat regnum tuum …'

Would he come to the Kingdom of God if he fell in battle?

'… et dimitte nobis debita nostra.'

Would God forgive his many sins and misdeeds? He thought about how he cowardly hid in the cellar while his father died alone in the battle against the Vikings. Was Gaius in heaven? Would he forgive him? Marcus thought of the promise he had made to Julia, that he would come and find her. Was she also in heaven, or suffering in a living hell with Torgils? Would Ulv find her?

'Et ne nos inducas in tentationem …'

He heard soft footsteps, which stopped right in front of him.

'… sed libera nos a malo.'

Marcus prayed for salvation from evil, to be spared from the man who was ready to take his life. He closed his eyes tighter and raised his voice:

'Amen'

***

-

Printed in Great Britain
by Amazon